The complete book of

AUTOMOBILE
BODY
DESIGN

The complete book of

AUTOMOBILE BODY DESIGN

Ian Beattie

ISBN 0 85429 217 9

First published March 1977

The Haynes Publishing Group
Sparkford Yeovil Somerset BA22 7JJ England

a FOULIS Motoring book

Printed by J H Haynes and Company Limited Sparkford Yeovil Somerset BA22 7JJ
Bound by Cedric Chivers Limited Bath Avon
Editor Tim Parker
Jacket design Phill Jennings

All the line illustrations by the author

Dedication

For **John,** valued friend of thirty years standing, and **George,** whose enthusiasm for elderly cars has proved infectious

Contents

Introduction

This work was conceived whilst browsing through several publications whose pages were graced by a large number of photographs of chiefly coachbuilt motor cars; amongst the information presented in the captions accompanying the photographs were details of the body types with which the various chassis had been fitted. It struck me that whilst every historic-car enthusiast knows what is meant by and forms a distinct mental image when confronted with such terms as *tourer* or *landaulette,* there is a sizable and complicated series of body designations that convey little or no instantaneous impression, for three principal reasons: firstly owing to sheer obscurity, secondly through the addition of qualifying yet ambiguous adjectives to relatively well-known terms, for instance *single phaeton,* and thirdly due to the appearance of two definitive terms in superficially incongruous juxtaposition, as in the case of *coupe limousine.*

To compound the apparent complexity of bodywork terminology many coachbuilders at one time or another utilised inept terms, and frequently applied freakish titles to their more unusual designs; it is in an endeavour to unscramble these, as well as the bewildering array of more orthodox designations, to which this work is overridingly devoted.

In Part I as many as possible of the manifold body types, whether generic, derivative or contrived, that have been created by both coachbuilders and automobile manufacturers throughout the close on one hundred year history of the horseless carriage, have been collated and described together with contextual comments on their respective origins and usages.

As the halcyon era of motor coachcraft becomes ever remoter and the number of personnel connected with, or experienced in, coachbuilding inevitably dwindles owing to the passage of time, the chance of losing our heritage in respect of motor bodywork knowledge from that and previous eras grows increasingly real, the recognition of which fact has acted as a persistent spur in my efforts to research and pen this survey.

10

Introduction

In terms of quality and output the heyday of the coachbuilt motor car was indisputably the twenty years bridging the two World Wars, therefore it should come as no surprise that most of the bodywork variations arise from that period; for that reason also the larger percentage of the illustrations herein have been taken from designs of those years.

Illustrations play a vitally important role in the structure of this work. However illuminative an author's descriptive powers may be it is seldom easy to communicate veritably graphic pictures in a somewhat esoteric subject such as this by verbal means alone, especially in consideration of those readers who may not be fully conversant with the broad outline of motor bodies at any one stage in automobile history. Therefore, reference to relevant illustrations is essential for truly satisfactory comprehension. Side-view line drawings are used here in preference to photographs; the latter could be employed in a survey of this nature, though to seek out a set of suitable and preferably previously-unpublished photographs of consistent size, quality and subjective position (ie side profile) is a well-nigh impossible undertaking. Because much of this survey is concerned with comparison, one body type or style to another, simplified two-dimensional drawings in which design facets may be highlighted (and, conversely, extraneous details toned down or deleted) fulfil the requisite degree of clarity and ease of comparability which photographs, however good, cannot achieve so effectively.

Since the genesis and subsequent progress of automotive bodywork was so intimately linked with the coachbuilding industry it is appropriate that some notion of the latter's influence should be expressed, as an adjunct to Part I. To this end I have selected for Part II a portfolio of designs emanating from fifty-five British, European and American coachbuilders, of which many are reasonably familiar whilst a number are but little-known outside their countries of origin; the illustrations serve to underline the extensive spectrum and ingenuity of body types and styles that coachbuilders were capable of offering to their fortunate clients. Complementary to these illustrations, Part II also contains brief biographical details on each of the featured coachbuilding concerns.

The final part, Part III, traces via text and illustrations the evolution in design over several decades of ten representative body types, all but two of which are very much extant today.

Except where demanded for an accurate description of a body type or design, I have not sought to cover the methods of construction or materials used on coachbuilt or mass-produced motor cars, since these aspects have already been amply enlarged upon elsewhere.

Ian Beattie   11

Notes on terminology

Consistent use is made herein of four particular terms that denote precisely defined periods in the history of the motor car which, in addition, act as qualifying adjectives for those cars fabricated within those periods. Whilst these terms are familiar to motoring enthusiasts in general, they are frequently misused or misapplied by the latter and especially so by the media (the press, radio and television), therefore an analytical restatement of these terms is desirable:

Veteran   the period from the dawn of motoring up till and including the year 1904,

Edwardian   the period from 1905 until cessation of motor car construction due to the First World War (several plants, including all those in the United States, were not converted to war work until as late as 1916-17),

Vintage   the period from recommencement of automobile production in 1918-19 up till and including the year 1930,

Post-War   the period from recommencement of automobile production in 1945-46 thenceforward.

A further term, *post-vintage thoroughbred,* applies to 'thoroughbred' cars constructed from the termination of the Vintage period (1931) up till the outbreak of World War II, but since this present text does not deal exclusively with thoroughbred models the term is not utilised herein. Historically and chronologically the *Edwardian* period is something of a misnomer since King Edward VII died in 1910; however the effects of his reign were felt until the four years of war between 1914 and 1918, and hence the deliberate protraction of the period for the purposes of motoring history - and indeed general history also.

The body designation *coupe,* a French expression meaning 'cut' and previously utilised for a horse-drawn carriage, is spelt without the accent in the United States. It is used without the accent here.

Where an American body designation occurs in the text it is indicated as such by the letters US in parentheses before or following the designation.

Part 1
Automobile body identification

Automobile body design

The first motor cars to appear on the roads of Europe in the late 1880s and early 1890s were simple, spartan machines; many were of three-wheel configuration, few had any form of suspension system beyond the inherent resilience of wire-spoked wheels, tyres were composed of solid rubber, engines were mounted amidships or astern and passengers were accommodated on cycle saddles, upholstered benches or basket-work chairs. Where fitted, bodywork was minimal and afforded little protection against either road dirt or the elements.

These crude devices rapidly progressed in reliability and sophistication as mechanical inventiveness and manufacturing techniques advanced, and it was natural that existing horse-drawn carriage bodies should form the basis of the earliest automobile bodies. The considerable number of companies extant at the turn of the century, whose collective expertise in carriage construction had matured over several centuries, began to apply their creative talents to motor chassis, the consequence being that carriage nomenclature was transposed from the age of the horse to the new age of the internal combustion engine. Hence the derivation of body type appellations.

As motor cars continued to develop during the first decade of the 20th Century, through the Edwardian era and into the 1920s the variety of divergent body types grew apace, at least in regard to those offered by coachbuilders, so that by the year 1930 the range of available body types was probably wider than at any time before or since.

The vast majority of coachbuilding concerns became extinct either during the 1930s as a result of the Great Depression and the ensuing economic backwash, or after the onset of peace in 1945 when money, materials and skilled labour were all in short supply. Repressive vehicle taxation laws hastened the end of many highly-respected European 'carrossiers' in the late 1940s, and the 1950s witnessed a further decline as the cost of craftsmanship rose steeply. Several formerly autonomous English coachbuilders were absorbed into the motor industry and either continued for a more or less limited period to build individual bodies or were totally ingested, thereby becoming mere links in the mass-production chain of assembly; other old-established coachbuilding companies were transformed into retail outlets whilst the remaining handful channelled their energies into production of specialist vehicles such as taxi-cabs and motor caravans.

The effect of this long-term reversal of coachbuilding fortunes, endorsed by radical changes in the established social structure spawned by the First World War and which gathered increasing momentum following the Second World War, together with the more recent policies of product rationalisation carried out by major motor manufacturers, has been to undermine and dilute the multiformity of body types. In one respect this has proved to have been an advantage in that the mass-production of a strictly limited variation of patterns is a primary factor in keeping the retail price of a motor car within reasonable bounds; a modern coachbuilt car may be more individualistic and is certainly better finished, but it is extremely expensive and yet - a Philistine viewpoint perhaps - it performs the basic functions required of an automobile no better than its mass-produced counterpart.

To achieve a semblance of order and progression the body types have been collated and classified into eight specific groups or sections.

There are, however, a number of body types which do not readily fall into any one of these groups; for the sake of simplicity each has been allocated to that group whose general characteristics it most closely resembles. Where applicable, American equivalents are appended above the descriptive passages.

To commence with, a list of important and characteristic bodywork fixtures and adornments is included, under the title Features and Fitments.

FEATURES AND FITMENTS

There are numerous bodywork characteristics and appurtenances, some of a general and others of a specialist nature, that require a measure of explanation, both for the sake of completeness but chiefly because many are used consistently in the main text. Unless they assume a new identification in coachbuilding nomenclature, familiar fixtures and fittings (windscreen, bonnet, mudguards or wings, etc) have been omitted, since it is taken for granted that the reader has at least a basic knowledge of the parts that go towards the making of a motor car. Of the items that follow, many were common to mass-produced cars as well as the coachbuilt variety, though only a handful of the terms are still in current usage.

The items are divided into three categories: firstly those common to or employed in the design at one period or another of both open and closed bodywork, secondly those pertaining to open cars alone, and thirdly those found only on closed cars.

GENERAL – BOTH OPEN AND CLOSED CARS

Chassis
The chassis supplied by a manufacturer to a coachbuilder was a complete car in all respects bar the bodywork and seats, so that a chassis fitted with a temporary driver's seat could be test-run on the road to diagnose and correct any problems that might arise before attachment of the body. Most makes of chassis were so tested before departure from the manufacturers. The majority of manufacturers supplied bonnets with their chassis as compulsory

items, and several manufacturers - notably Duesenberg in the United States - delivered chassis complete with wings.

Compartment

In a four-seater or larger body the interior is physically divided into two sections or compartments by a partition or division, or simply by the presence of the front seats.

Legroom

A significant factor of the rear compartment insofar as most bodies are concerned, the legroom is the amount of space available from the forward edge of the seat cushion to the nearest obstruction, be it the front seat back, division or suchlike. In, for instance, a very close-coupled four-seater coupe the rear legroom may be so parsimonious that the 'room for one's legs' is indeed restricted to the anatomical minimum - or even less.

Light

A light is a side or door window. The descriptive term 'four-light', for example, signifies that a body contains two windows per side, four in total excluding the windscreen and rear window; the latter is frequently referred to as a *back* or *rear light*. To avoid confusion lighting accessories were invariably called Head*lamps,* Driving *lamps,* etc, in coachbuilding nomenclature.

Quarter Panel

The quarter or rear-quarter panel is that panel above the body waistline situated between the back panel and the door window (rear door window on a four-door body) on either side of the car. In a body with a folding hood the quarter panel is part of the hood and consequently folds with it.

Quarter Light

Otherwise termed a rear-quarter light, this is a window inserted in the quarter panel. In modern parlance the small pivoted window located immediately behind the windscreen pillar and used for ventilation purposes is also referred to as a quarter light (strictly speaking a front-quarter light) and by other epithets such as *vent wing* and *vent window,* though with the introduction and subsequent refinement of internal, integral ventilation systems this window is fast disappearing as a general fitment. However, the older definition of quarter light is tacit wherever the term appears in this text.

Back Panel

The back, rear or (where applicable) tail panel is the transverse panel at the rear of the body. In the days before large enclosed boots came into fashion the back panel extended from the roofline to the base of the body and incorporated the rear window; on the older open car the rearmost panel of the folding hood thus constituted part of the back panel. Nowadays the back panel is normally taken to be that panel below the boot lid against which the bumper is mounted, although the term is still occasionally utilised to denote the panel containing the rear light, behind the rear seats.

Turn-under
Turn-under was the term used to denote the inward curve of body or door panels from the waistline downwards.

Waistline
The waistline of a body corresponds with an imaginary line located just below the side or door windows and extended over the length of the body. In very many instances the waistline is delineated by a narrow painted or plated strip.

Scuttle *(US: Cowl)*
The scuttle is the area of bodywork between the rear of the bonnet and the windscreen.

Hinge Pillar
The vertical frame pillar on which a door is hung.

Shut Pillar
The vertical frame pillar against which a door shuts.

Cant Rail
This is a horizontal rail on either side of the car which extends from the windscreen pillar rearwards above the doors in order to support the roof. In the case of a folding hood the cant rails are integral with the collapsible hood framework.

Composite Construction
The construction of a body utilising timber framework clad with sheet-steel, aluminium or light-alloy panels.

Close-coupled, Short-coupled
Both terms denote bodywork in which the front and rear rows of seats are set close together to achieve a comparatively short body.

Formal Body
A body of generally staid yet imposing lines, designed to be chauffeur-driven and intended for use on formal occasions.

17

Automobile body design

Foursome
This term simply denotes the provision of seating for four people within a body.

Division *(US: Partition)*
The division is a glass panel that separates the front and rear compartments in a formal body. It is lowered manually or electrically, for communication purposes, into a well behind the front seats; alternatively a sliding division - two glass panels that slide horizontally one behind the other - may be specified, as in this form a bulky well is unnecessary. Early closed coachwork frequently included a division hinged at its upper edge that could be raised and fastened to the underside of the front compartment roof.

Partition
A partition is a permanent timber or metal panel mounted behind the front seats to the height of the seat backs in order to actively separate the front and rear compartments. Some early forms of closed coachwork featured stationary glass panels in place of movable divisions, in which case the entire structure from floor to roof was called a partition. Many open touring bodies were fitted with partitions either as a basis for a half-deck or to house occasional seats. Partition was but rarely utilised as a synonym for division, except in the United States.

Occasional Seats
Variously known as auxiliary, extra or (in latterday nomenclature) jump seats, these are collapsible seats located in the rear compartment directly behind the division or partition; they can be neatly folded away when not required. Occasional seats are generally supplied in pairs or threes and mounted facing forward, although sideways-facing occasional seats were quite common at one time and especially so in less spacious rear compartments.

Dickey Seat *(US: Rumble Seat)*
Very popular during the Vintage era, the dickey seat was a folding seat incorporated in the tail of two-seater cars, accommodating one or two passengers.

de Ville
The addition of this term to a body type, eg limousine de ville, indicated the provision of an opening roof over the front compartment that could be folded up or slid back into the roof covering the rear compartment. Literally 'of town', the de ville front was largely restricted to formal bodies only.

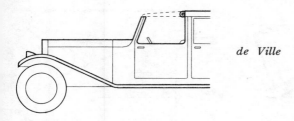

de Ville

Sedanca

The word sedanca when appended to a coupe-body type, eg drop-head sedanca coupe, indicated that a de ville front was furnished with that body. In this context sedanca was synonymous with de ville and was not used as such excepting in connection with coupe styles; the perplexingly-titled sedanca de ville body was one in which the term sedanca indicated a large saloon.

Sidescreen

Utilised principally on open-bodied cars, in sets of at least two depending on body configuration, a sidescreen was a detachable door or side window comprising a fabric-covered wire frame surrounding a panel of flexible transparent material, usually celluloid.

Side Curtain

Mostly fitted in front compartments of open drive bodies, a side curtain was a curtain of isinglass or celluloid normally kept rolled up in the roof and unfurled to provide some measure of side protection against inclement weather.

Kamm Tail

The Kamm tail comprises a foreshortened vertical or near-vertical rear panel, a structure being one of the conclusions reached by Prof. W.E. Kamm after an in-depth investigation into automobile aerodynamics, carried out with the aid of a wind tunnel at Stuttgart during the 1930s.

Kamm propounded that the theoretically ideal elongated, tapered tail and a sharply abbreviated tail differed minimally in aerodynamic drag induced at high speed; in practice a tapered tail is an unwieldy protrusion, whereas the Kamm-inspired rear is neat and has proved highly successful.

Initially introduced on selected BMWs for the curtailed 1940 Mille Miglia, the Kamm tail has been widely utilised since the mid-1950s.

OPEN CARS

Boat-tailed

This referred to a touring body the tail of which was shaped to simulate the prow of a boat.

Automobile body design

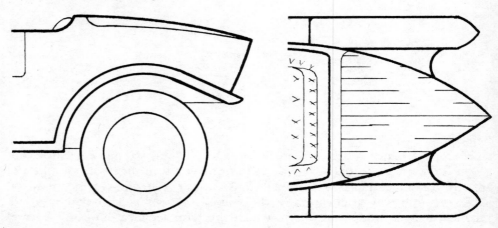

Boat-Tail

Boat-decked
This term referred to a body the top panel (deck) of whose tail was overlaid with or constructed of timber slats in a similar manner to the deck of a boat. This form of decking was most frequently coupled with boat-tailed bodies.

Barrel-sided
This refers to the shape of an open touring body which, when viewed from front or rear, exhibits pronouncedly convex-curved side and door panels together with a fair degree of turn-under. This curvature is considered to equate very approximately to or is at least reminiscent of that displayed by the common-or-garden wooden barrel, and hence the term.

A term more popular nowadays than ever it was in the heyday of motor coachbuilding, it is associated with certain open touring designs of the 1920s.

Fishtail *(US)*
A fishtail body was a body in which the tail was a longer, slimmer version of the boat-tail.

Cloverleaf
A term for a three-seater tourer, the single rear seat of which was mounted centrally behind the front seats. In plan view the arrangement was reminiscent of the three-leafed clover and hence the name.

Beetleback
A tail composed of generously-rounded panels that bore a passing resemblance to the carapace of a beetle.

Duckback
The duckback was a slim, pointed tail which was sharply undercut on a reverse slope, the whole suggestive of a duck's nether regions. The Duckback Alvis 12/50 Tourer is the most famous example of the use of this feature.

Toast-rack
This was a four-seater four-door touring body with door apertures from which doors were omitted; hence the soubriquet.

Cape Cart Hood
Derived from the small horsedrawn South African cape cart, the cape cart hood was the standard touring car hood from the earliest days of motoring until around 1930, when the name was dropped, comprising a roof section, back panel and collapsible timber or metal frame. In early nomenclature a cape cart hood *per se* encompassed a single row of seats only and an Extended cape cart hood two rows. Quarter panels were added as part of the hood fabric for those open bodies equipped with glass door windows, as opposed to sidescreens.

Victoria Hood
A folding hood of triangular side aspect originally fitted to horsedrawn Victorias, it was used in this form on early motor car bodies, but the name came to be utilised for a hood designed for two-door two-light cars with generous quarter panels as part of the hood structure.

Three-position Hood
This was a folding hood that could be manoeuvred into three positions, namely: fully erected, de ville, and fully collapsed.

Hardtop (detachable)
Not to be confused with the full body style of the same name (qv saloon section), a detachable hardtop is a metal or glass-fibre structure comprising a roof panel, rear window and quarter panels - in some instances containing quarter lights - which fits snugly over the passenger area of a convertible or open sports car. It may be attached or removed at will, and is designed as a supplementary, 'winter-wear' item to the standard folding hood fitted to such models.

Targa Top
So named after the Porsche Targa introduced in 1966 in which this feature was first exploited (apart from a brief excursion on a similar theme by Triumph on a TR4 variant in 1961-1962 when it was called a surrey top!), the targa top differs from a detachable hardtop in that the roof panel alone

Automobile body design

is removable, the rear window and quarter panels being part of the basic body structure. The metal or glass-fibre roof is generally designed to be carried in the boot upon removal, otherwise a temporary flexible panel for use against sudden inclement weather may be provided.

This easily-convertible and most effective arrangement combines the functions of both hood and hardtop in the simplest possible manner (a folding hood is not, indeed cannot be fitted to a car equipped with a targa top), and its application is growing apace amongst the manufacturers of sporting cars.

Power-operated hood

This is a hood ('top', 'soft-top' or 'rag-top' in North America) that is raised and lowered by means of an electro-hydraulic mechanism. Fitted to all American convertibles since World War II, power-operated hoods are fairly rare on British and Continental models.

Hood-, Landau-, S-irons

These were hinged, s-shaped external brackets mounted on both sides of a hood that held the latter in tension when erected. They were also fashionable at times as non-functional adornments on closed bodies.

Half-deck *(US: Dual-cowl, twin-cowl)*

Very fashionable during the 1920s and 1930s, the half-deck was a deck that partially covered the rear compartment of an open tourer. In the closed position it lay flush with the body sides and door tops; hinged to a partition behind the front seats it could be swung upwards to facilitate access to the rear seats. The half-deck was frequently surmounted by an auxiliary (Auster) windscreen or aero screens.

Aero Screen

A small rectangular or semi-circular windscreen found on sporting cars, normally mounted in pairs behind a fold-flat windscreen. Aero screens were originally developed for racing cars.

Tonneau Cover

This is a detachable waterproof cover fastened over the seating area, part of which can be opened to expose the driving seat and controls, or alternatively both front seats, with the remainder in place.

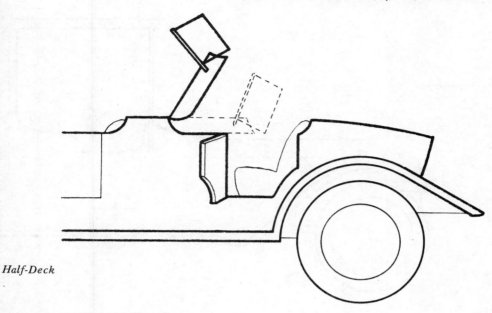

Half-Deck

CLOSED CARS

Open Drive

This term implied that the driver's compartment in a formal body was open to the elements through the lack of side or door windows. Whilst a roof and windscreen were generally provided, it was quite common for an open drive body to be designed without a front compartment roof, and occasionally with neither roof nor windscreen. Nevertheless the criterion of an open drive car was essentially the deliberate omission of front compartment side protection (side curtains were however sometimes specified) whatever the varying arrangements of roof or windscreen.

Open drive as a feature began to lapse in popularity in bodies built from the mid-1920s onwards, being replaced by Enclosed Drive in the interests of driver comfort. *Open front* was an alternative though rarely-used epithet for open drive.

Enclosed Drive

Otherwise *Closed* or *Interior Drive,* this signified that as opposed to open drive the driver's compartment in a formal body was fully equipped with side glazing, affording total weather protection. The term was rendered superfluous and consequently became defunct after the late 1920s when closed body designs began to incorporate enclosed drive automatically.

23

Automobile body design

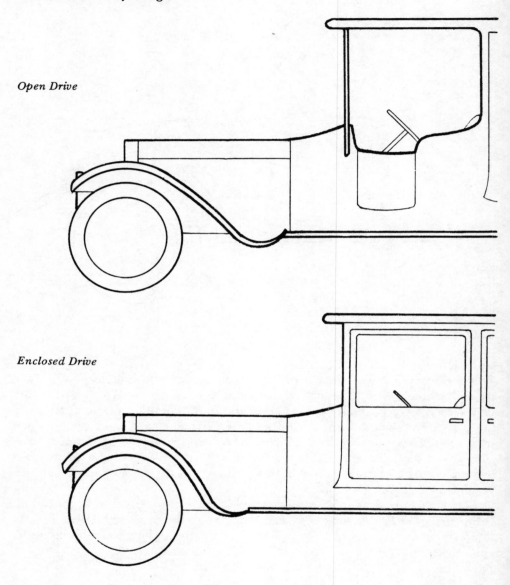

Open Drive

Enclosed Drive

D-front
A feature found in conjunction with open drive bodies only, a D-front was the forward panel structure of a rear compartment, ie a partition, embodying a glass division that was flanked by curved panels into which windows were inset. The D-front was so-called because in plan view the curvature of these panels imparted an elongated 'D' shape to the structure.

24

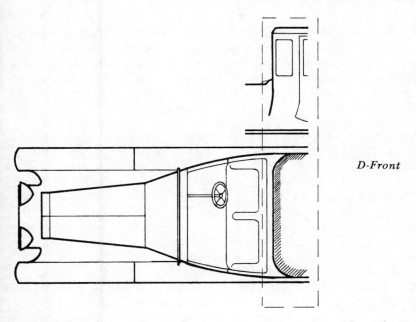

D-Front

Razor-edged
A razor-edged body was one in which the exterior edges and corners were sharply delineated.

Top-hat
This was an epithet applied to a saloon body in which that part of the body above the waistline was designed with a vertical emphasis; in conjunction with razor-edged or crisply-rendered panels this resulted in a distinctive, 'cuboid' appearance.

Pullman
Pullman was frequently appended to saloons and limousines to promote an air of superior luxury, such as was associated with the celebrated Pullman railway coaches.

Special
Appended to a formal body type this term signified either that the body was furnished with unusual appointments to the stipulation of the customer, or that the body was a one-off design.

In another sense a special was a one-off car, usually comprising a number of proprietary components, constructed by an individual or manufacturer for a particular task, be it competition work, experimental testing, or suchlike.

25

Automobile body design

Fastback
An American term that has found its way into common English usage, fastback can indicate either a body feature or less commonly a complete body style. It refers to a coupe-type body in which the roof panel slopes gently downwards in an unbroken line from a point above the rear seats to the rear panel.

Hatchback
Having only come into fashionable use over the past three years or so, this term denotes the provision on a fastback or semi-fastback saloon, or four-seater fixed-head coupe, of a large lifting rear door that encompasses not only the rear window but also what would otherwise be the boot lid. Additionally, a hatchback saloon (or coupe) is furnished with estate car-type folding rear seats, so that such a car represents an intermediary stage between the conventional saloon or coupe and the traditional form of estate car; the presence of the fastback roof however does detract from the available loading volume relative to that of an equivalent estate car.

Their versatility combined with more curvaceous lines than the comparatively square-rigged appearance of most estate cars has attracted ever-growing popularity; the species originated with the Renault 16, now well beyond its tenth year in full production, followed by the Austin Maxi in 1968 and latterly by a host of such models of both 3- and 5-door format. The Mark II version of the Ford Capri is an example of a hatchback coupe, whilst the clean-lined Vauxhall Chevette is typical of the latest generation of hatchback saloons.

Notchback *(US)*
Conceived by American auto buffs in the early 1960s, the term Notchback was originally utilised to denote an automobile body featuring a reversed-slope rear window, in the manner of the English Ford Anglia and Classic models produced during that period; the more or less acute angle formed between the profiled rear window line and the adjacent boot deck gave rise to the notion of a 'notch' effect. When this design fell out of favour the term was discontinued, yet it was partially resurrected in the United States around 1970 in order to meet the description of a styling characteristic that struck a mean between the normal, straightforward rear window/boot deck configuration and the full fastback style, where the rear window line meets the boot panel at a very shallow angle on a body which otherwise appears very much akin to a fastback.

Sunshine Roof
Or *Sun Roof,* this is a metal or fabric panel covering an aperture in the roof of a body; it is opened by a sliding or folding action to admit sunlight and/or fresh air.

Opera Window *(US)*
This is a small quarter light mounted each side of the body either directly behind the rear-most door light as per a conventional quarter light, or isolated in a central position in the quarter panel. In the latter case the opera window may be other than a rectangular shape - circular or oval, for instance.

EARLY NOMENCLATURE

With a few notable exceptions all the body types listed in this section pertain to cars built from the dawn of motoring until 1904, the end of the Veteran era.

The huge majority of very early cars entertained no form of weather protection whatsoever apart from mudguards; windscreens and simple hoods began to make an appearance at the turn of the century, but full-length collapsible hoods and solid roofs, side curtains and glazed windows did not become general till much later.

Tricar
Several of the very earliest, prototype internal-combustion engined devices were constructed on the three-wheel principle in a similar pattern to a pedal tricycle. They were based on cycle-type tubular frames, utilised cycle saddles and were indeed little more than motorised tricycles. These simple three-wheeled horseless carriages were called tricars.

Produced sporadically over a period of some twenty-five years up to 1910 or thereabouts, tricars remained exiguous, uncomplicated machines that were little developed beyond their experimental forebears except that the wheel configuration was normally reversed from the tricycle principle - ie the single wheel displaced to the rear - to improve stability.

Many makes of three-wheeled cars were introduced after 1910, notably Morgan, indeed there are still three-wheelers in production today, but they were not strictly tricars, the word being reserved specifically for the crude three-wheelers of the early motoring era. Probably the best-known example of a tricar in this country is the Riley Tricar of 1904.

Forecar
This was a car of the Veteran era whose front seat was situated between or ahead of the front wheels, a highly vulnerable position for its occupant who acted as the principal energy-absorber in a frontal impact! However the driver was placed amidships in comparative safety above or forward of the engine. A forecar could be of either three or four-wheel construction, and several manufacturers built forecars to accommodate three or more people.

27

Automobile body design

Tandem

A tandem was a two-seater tricar whose occupants were placed one behind the other in tandem fashion, the device being controlled from the rear. In most instances the driver was supplied with a cycle-type saddle whilst the passenger rode in rather greater comfort in a chair of basketwork or similar lightweight material; similarly to a forecar, the passenger was positioned between the front wheels.

Many tricars were of tandem configuration, however the name tandem was but rarely applied in lieu of tricar.

Vis-a-vis

A vis-a-vis was a four-wheeled car suitable for four or more occupants in which the two rows of seats faced each other, the driver situated in the forward-facing rear seat. Obvious and inherently rather dangerous problems of impaired driver visibility arose when a full complement of passengers was carried; nonetheless this type of car was fairly popular in the early days of motoring when roads were empty, probably because many horsedrawn carriages were of vis-a-vis form.

A body type in its own right, vis-a-vis strictly speaking simply denoted the seating arrangement (being French for 'face-to-face').

Dos-a-dos

The dos-a-dos was a car for four or more persons in which the two rows of seats were mounted back to back (dos-a-dos means exactly that in French); the driver in this instance was seated in the front and therefore experienced none of the problems associated with the vis-a-vis.

In a similar manner to vis-a-vis, dos-a-dos was used either as a body type per se or as an indication of the seating arrangement in other body styles.

Dog-Cart

This is a term that is almost indefinable, since it was seemingly applied at random to two, four or six-seater cars with dos-a-dos or straightforward seating formations. In general, dog-carts were tall and fitted with large road wheels, in many instances the driven rear wheels being of greater diameter than the front wheels.

Voiturette

Voiturette is a French word derived from *Voiture,* the standard French term for a vehicle or motor car: the addition of *ette* produces a diminutive of the original word, thus a voiturette was a light car and as such was any small car with a relatively low engine displacement and power output. The term arose in the Veteran era and was used consistently into the 1930s, very often in connection with a class of racing car of lighter construction and lower power than the topline grand prix models. An example of a racing voiturette of the 1930s is the supercharged ERA single-seater, which was raced in a different category to the immensely powerful Grand Prix Mercedes-Benz and Auto Unions of the same period.

Spider, Spyder
A spider was originally a very light and somewhat spindly horse-drawn conveyance, so that when the motor car began to appear on the scene the term spider came to be associated with a lightweight two-seater car. An extempore third seat mounted at the rear was occasionally fitted to those spiders of sufficient length to accommodate one.

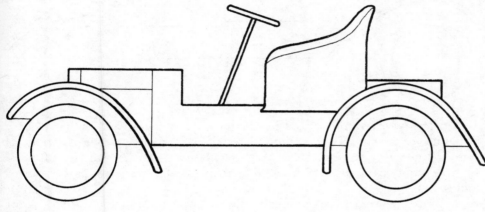

Spider

Victoria
Tracing its origins to a horse-drawn carriage of the same name, the victoria was a comparatively light two-seater car that was frequently equipped with a folding hood, appropriately enough a victoria hood.

Surrey
Another body type derived directly from a carriage, the surrey was a light four-seater car often fitted with a full-length canopy which generally proved to be more decorative than protective.

Tonneau
In later years called a *Rear-Entrance* or *Hind-Entrance* tonneau to distinguish it from its derivative the side-entrance tonneau, this was a four-seater car in which the individual rear seats were placed in the rear corners of the body and accessible via a door let into the back panel.

29

Automobile body design

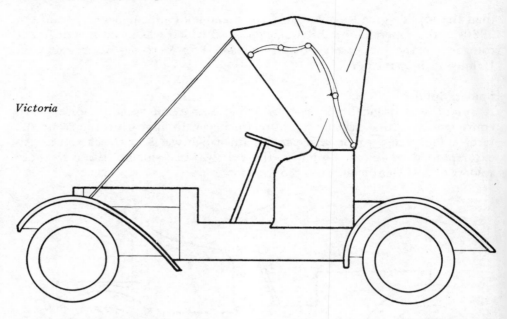

Victoria

The word *tonneau* is French, meaning a wine cask or barrel of a particular capacity and is still used as such in wine-growing districts of France; the word came to be applied to a body style through the shape of the rear compartment, which resembled a 'half-tonneau' on early touring bodies.

The rear-entrance tonneau was a very fashionable body in the Veteran era and comparatively large numbers were manufactured. A goodly proportion of competing cars in the annual Veteran London to Brighton Run are rear-entrance tonneaux, which attests to its popularity in its heyday.

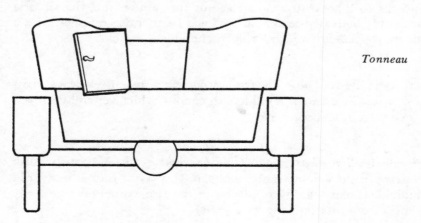

Tonneau

Double Tonneau

A tonneau accommodating four people in the rear compartment, by the addition of two rear-facing seats mounted directly behind the driving and front passenger's seats.

Phaeton, Tonneau Phaeton

A phaeton was a sprightly horse-drawn carriage; the name was applied to early motor bodies and phaeton and tonneau became interchangeable titles, thus the phaeton or tonneau phaeton was synonymous with the rear-entrance tonneau.

Buggy *(US)*

Buggy was a designation utilised almost exclusively in the United States to denote a very light, spartan two-seater of simple but rugged construction, in the manner of its horse-drawn forebear.

High-Wheeler *(US)*

Indigenous to the United States, the high-wheeler was a buggy equipped with especially tall, slender solid-tyred wheels to negotiate the deeply rutted tracks which passed for highways in that country at the beginning of the century. This primitive machine was still in production towards the end of the Edwardian era - long past obsolescence - since few backwood regions were even then served by metalled roads.

TOURER

Tourer *(US: Touring Car)*

Tourer was the generic title for an open car offering accommodation for at least four people with access to the seats via two, three or four doors. Weather-protective equipment normally comprised a full-length folding hood and detachable sidescreens or curtains, though purchasers could opt for greater or lesser degrees of weatherproofing - some hardy souls taking it to the point where even a windscreen was shunned. Pre-World War I tourers tended towards frugality of such equipment, chiefly through lack of development of such fittings.

As may be seen from the ensuing descriptions in this section, there were many and varied types of open touring car, yet all are by definition tourers - a rose by any other name, as it were. The touring body was exceedingly popular throughout the Edwardian and Vintage epochs, after which time the closed saloon-type body rose to prominence as mass-production techniques improved, prices were lowered or stabilised and cars became more numerous.

Apt examples of touring bodies combining both purpose and

31

Automobile body design

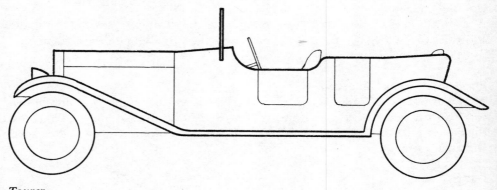

Tourer

elegance were those constructed on Bentley 3-litre and 4½-litre chassis by the English coachbuilder Vanden Plas during the 1920s.

Sports Tourer
The sports tourer was fundamentally a tourer of sporting lines, and many sports touring bodies were augmented by sleek, flared wings. Often, however, a straightforward tourer was termed a sports model in order to increase its showroom appeal.

Side-Entrance Tonneau
Alternatively the *Side-Entrance Phaeton,* this body was a direct development of the rear-entrance tonneau. During the first four or so years of this century technical progress had advanced sufficiently to enable wheelbases to be lengthened, thus allowing the adoption of side doors in lieu of rear-entry; hence the appellation side-entrance.

Within very few years of its emergence this body type came to be known as the tourer, so that the term side-entrance tonneau effectively bridged the gap between the old rear-entrance tonneau and the standard tourer, the former owing much of its design to the horse-drawn carriage era whilst the latter was the first to utilise bodywork specifically conceived for the motor car chassis.

Torpedo, Torpedo Tourer
Frequently termed a *Flush-sided Phaeton* in pre-1914 coachwork nomenclature, a torpedo was a tourer distinguished by a body line of constant height from the scuttle rearwards, atop the body sides and doors onto the back panel. In order to accentuate the smooth appearance of the car the seat back tops were so mounted to coincide with the height of the body sides.

The torpedo was a very fashionable style just before the First World

32

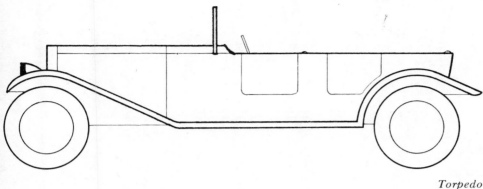

Torpedo

War and during the 1920s, giving rise to some superb creations from a variety of British and European coachbuilders.

Sports Torpedo
In a manner similar to the relationship of the tourer to the sports tourer, the sports torpedo exhibited eminently sporting and sometimes rakish lines, generally in conjunction with flared or streamlined wings, the visual success of the latter depending on both the 'aesthetic eye' of the designer and the fashion of the day.

Skiff
A comparatively rare type of motor car body, the skiff was a two or four-seater sports tourer or torpedo whose carefully swept lines suggested its lissom water-borne namesake. The most famous skiff body of all time was that constructed and clad in timber and mounted on a Panhard and Levassor chassis by Henri Labourdette of Paris in 1913 for the pioneer racing motorist Chevalier Rene de Knyff.

Phaeton
Just as the phaeton of the Veteran era was synonymous with the tonneau, the latterday phaeton was identical in all practical respects to the tourer, although the phaeton came to be imbued with a rather more sporting flavour and therefore could equally well be termed a sports tourer. Being a foursome body it was definitively a *Double Phaeton* (qv) though the qualification double was deemed inherent and therefore dropped by most coachbuilders.

Phaeton bodies were noted for their elegance; many were equipped with a half-deck and auxiliary rear-compartment windscreen that enhanced the sporting character. Whilst the style went out of favour in the United Kingdom during the late 1920s it underwent a rejuvenation in the United States at that time, notably on model J and SJ Duesenberg chassis. **33**

Automobile body design

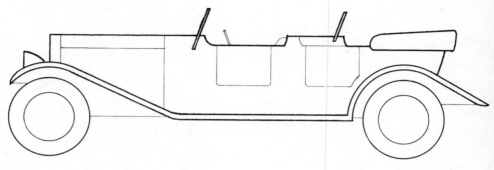

Phaeton

Single Phaeton
The single phaeton was a sporting two-seater of considerable panache whose seats were arranged side-by-side in the usual fashion, ie in a single row - and hence the qualification 'single'.

Double Phaeton
A double phaeton, more commonly known simply as a phaeton, was the most familiar of the three styles of phaeton bodywork; it was equipped with four seats mounted in two rows and often sported a half-deck in addition (vide phaeton).

Triple Phaeton
This was an exceedingly rare body that was especially designed to contain six seats in three rows. The triple phaeton was of necessity a very large vehicle and therefore somewhat unwieldy even on the emptiest of highways, however should a customer have desired a six-seater phaeton the coachbuilders' solution was generally to advise the provision of occasional seats within the shorter double phaeton body. The presence of such seats in a double phaeton did not on the other hand qualify it as a triple phaeton, since each row of seats in the latter were permanently secured and moreover served by individual access doors.

Torpedo Phaeton
A torpedo phaeton was identical to and synonymous with the torpedo tourer (qv).

Sport Phaeton *(US)*
This aptly-named American body style was a foursome tourer built on substantially rakish lines together with, though by no means invariably, a boat- or semi-boat-tail.

Protected Phaeton
Seldom found after the mid-1920s, the protected phaeton was a double phaeton equipped with a full-length solid roof in the style of and in place of the customary folding cape cart hood.

Roi des Belges, Tulip Phaeton
A late-Veteran and Edwardian style named after King Leopold II of the Belgians who had commissioned such a design from Carrossiers Rothschild of Paris in 1902, the roi des belges was a commodious open car featuring tall, high-set seats - especially the rear seat - and broad body sides. The original but subsequently secondary title of tulip phaeton was derived from the characteristic shape and turn-under of the back panel, which bore a passing resemblance to the vertically-bisected outline of a tulip.

Whilst it was well-suited to large weighty chassis of the Silver Ghost Rolls-Royce genre, the compound curves of the roi des belges body were difficult to render effectively on smaller chassis, so that although several leading coachbuilders achieved considerable aesthetic success with their interpretations there was an abundance of roi des belges bodies that were bulky, ungainly and scarcely elegant.

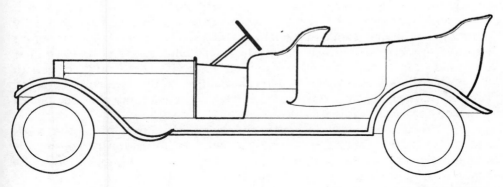

Roi des Belges

Sporting Victoria
A rather impractical form of bodywork that was chiefly mounted on Hispano-Suiza, Isotta Fraschini and suchlike chassis for the wealthy entrants of fashionable concours d'elegance in France and elsewhere during the 1920s, the sporting victoria was a sports torpedo or phaeton to which was attached a fixed or folding carriage-style, triangular-aspect victoria hood covering the rear seats only, the front seats remaining unprotected from prevailing weather conditions.

Emerging in 1910 or thereabouts, the total number of sporting victorias built was very small and it is unlikely that any have survived in their

Automobile body design

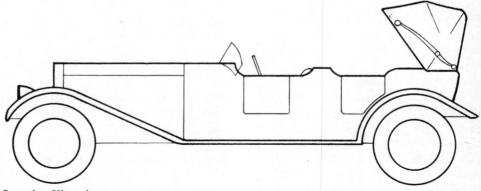

Sporting Victoria

original form, since concours d'elegance competitors tended to re-body their cars with bewildering frequency in the effort to outvie each other in initiating coachwork trends.

All-Weather Tourer *(US: Town Tourer)*

The all-weather tourer was a straightforward tourer in that it provided accommodation for four or more persons with access via two or more doors, but it was in the degree of weather protection that it differed most markedly with other tourers, supplied as it was with really effective and generous weather-protective equipment in the form of winding, lifting or fixed glass side and door windows in conjunction with a close-fitting, full-length collapsible hood. Pre-World War I all-weather tourers incorporated side curtains and certain early post-war examples sidescreens, but the principle of efficient weatherproofing was identical.

This was a body built in very considerable numbers during the 1920s and early 1930s - before the overall ascendency of saloon cars - since it successfully united the undoubted pleasures of open motoring with the superior comfort of a permanently closed car.

Coupe Sports Tourer

This was a contrived designation for an extremely rare type of coachbuilt Vintage body, a foursome sports tourer featuring individual folding hoods to both front and rear compartments; either hood could be raised or lowered independently of the other. The two compartments were divided by a partition surmounted by a fold-flat windscreen that provided attachment points for the erected rear hood.

Cyclecar

As its name implies, a cyclecar was a very light, highly exiguous and mechanically crude device in which motorcycle influences were brought to bear on much of its overall design, principally in the areas of engines utilised (generally aircooled single- or twin-cylinders) and transmission arrangements; drive to the differential-less rear axle and skimpy cycle-type wheels was effected via a single belt or chain.

The smallest cyclecars were single-seaters, though the majority of models were two-seaters of either tandem or side-by-side formation; the steering (controlled from the rear seat on many tandem examples, notably the Bedelia) was primitive, progressing from axle-pivot to wire-and-bobbin systems.

Developed as a bridging medium between the cheap but often inconvenient motorcycle and the much more expensive straightforward motor car, the species was extant over some twelve years from 1910, disappearing altogether on the emergence of mass-produced small cars during the early 1920s.

Roadster *(US: Roadster, Runabout, Raceabout, Speedster, Sportster)*

Seldom utilised beyond the late 1950s after a span of fifty years or more, the term roadster encompassed an almost infinite diversity of shapes, sizes, degrees of power and wealth of equipment. The criterion of a roadster body, however, was the provision of two seats only within a body of sporting lines, usually in conjunction with some form of folding hood, the latter frequently rather crude or unsightly when erected, since the raison d'etre of a roadster was the enjoyment of open motoring together with good performance and a high level of manoeuvrability.

Many early roadsters were exiguous in the extreme, an appropriate example being the American Mercer Raceabout of 1912, which was manufactured without a body and with merely a 'monocle' windscreen for the driver. Much later models, for instance the 1959 Jaguar XK150S, were not only very much better appointed but also - as one would expect in view of the forty-odd years of engine development - imbued with a far higher turn of speed.

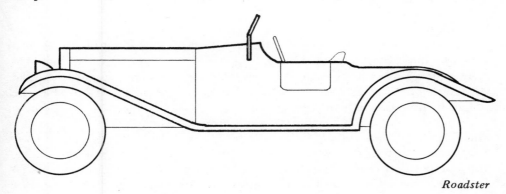

Roadster 37

Automobile body design

Two-Seater
Generally interchangeable with roadster and particularly popular in usage in this country before and after World War II, the title two-seater has come to be associated with two-seater sporting cars of relatively small exterior dimensions and engine displacement. To take a case in point, the BMW 328 of 1936-1939 was not only a roadster but also a two-seater and yet again a sports car (qv); all these terms describe the car in question and one takes one's choice as to which is used.

Coupe Roadster *(US)*, Convertible Roadster *(US)*, Sport Roadster *(US)*, Sports Roadster *(US)*
Broadly similar in concept, these four American roadster bodies were more luxurious than the general run of roadsters of the period (between the wars) and sported winding or lifting glass door windows in addition to close-fitting folding hoods.

Sports, Sports Car
Almost universally acknowledged as being exceedingly difficult, if not impossible to define, the term sports car embraces the entire gamut of open cars of the remotest sporting pretensions. Possibly the most meaningful definition of a sports car is any car that possesses the ability to impart a sense of exhilaration and joie-de-vivre to its driver.

In contemporary parlance a sports car approximates to a two or occasional-four seater open car of low build and sleek lines, though the modern closed equivalent called the *Gran Turismo* (or simply GT) may now also be accepted as a sports car. Unhappily the GT designation has been debased of late by misapplication to mass-produced saloons and even estate cars in the relentless pursuit of exclusivity.

Sport
Sport is the French, German and Italian equivalent of sports car.

Spider, Spyder
This is a very early motor bodywork designation that was revived after World War II and utilised consistently by Italian coachbuilders and motor manufacturers to signify an open two-seater sporting car, usually supplied with more or less adequate weather-protective equipment. Note that the Italian spelling should always be spider.

Single-Seater, Monoposto
Single-seater and monoposto are terms chiefly applied to Grand Prix, racing and competition cars of single-seat construction (Monoposto being Italian for *Single-Seat*). Until 1925 two-seater racing cars were mandatory, since the

regulations for most major events called for both the driver and a mechanic to be carried; thereafter single-seater cars were permitted and the appropriate terms came into existence.

COUPE

Coupe

A French word meaning 'cut' (with an accent on the 'e'), coupe was and still is the generic term for a relatively short two-door, two or four-light body containing two or four seats under either a fully-folding hood or a solid roof, coupled with winding or lifting glass door and side windows. Because coupe is such a comprehensive term the two distinct types of coupe bodywork, that fitted with a folding hood and the fixed roof style, are named *Drop-Head* and *Fixed-Head* coupe respectively, are both unusually succinct titles in comparison with most other bodywork designations.

The coupe in all its multiformity has been a consistently popular type of car ever since the first years of the motoring age and remains so today; a coupe was originally a form of horse-drawn carriage. The majority of modern coupes - to be precise, fixed-head coupes - are based largely on saloon bodies that have been adapted accordingly; an instance of this close kinship between saloon and coupe is the 1975 Ford Granada Ghia Saloon and Coupe, which are outwardly identical apart from the roofline and door arrangements (the coupe being two-door and the saloon four-door).

Several examples of coupe bodies of the 1920s and 1930s were not short in the conventional sense, in particular those mounted on very lengthy chassis such as Hispano-Suiza or 8-litre Bentley, but in comparison with their saloon or formal-bodied counterparts they were certainly close-coupled, and moreover their long tails permitted a very much larger volume of luggage to be carried when necessary.

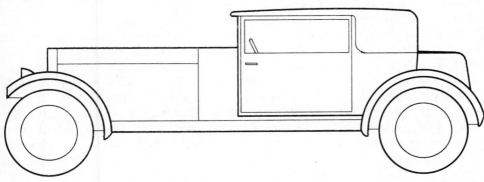

Automobile body design

Three-Quarter Coupe

Extant during the Edwardian and Vintage eras, the three-quarter coupe was a body that housed two seats only, in conjunction with a fairly voluminous tail into which a dickey seat was often inserted. This style incorporated small quarter lights behind the doors as standard fitments, and could be constructed with either a fixed roof or a collapsible hood; where the latter was specified the body was occasionally retitled as a *Three-Quarter Coupe Cabriolet* or (less euphonically) *Three-Quarter Cabriolet*.

Unless the design of this type of bodywork was handled carefully at the outset the proportions of the bonnet, passenger area and tail could be disastrous; as a basis of truly competent design and superb craftsmanship one need look no further than a Barker-bodied Rolls-Royce 20 Three-Quarter Coupe.

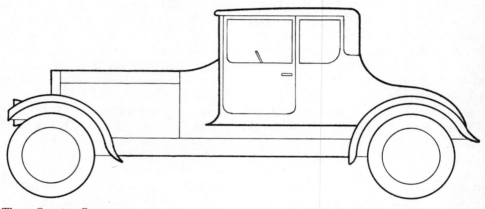

Three-Quarter Coupe

Sports Coupe, Sportsman's Coupe
Doctor's Coupe, Golfer's Coupe

These were four bodies of fundamentally similar concept and appearance and differing only in detail appointments to the three-quarter coupe; in parallel with the latter either fixed roofs or folding hoods were fitted, though, unlike the three-quarter coupe, drop-head versions of these bodies always retained the same designations as the fixed-head versions. In many instances these bodies were constructed without quarter lights.

The doctor's coupe in particular was a highly popular body, and many have survived. Why the doctor's coupe was so-called was probably that general practitioners found these compact and manoeuvrable cars afforded sufficient space for carriage of and easy access to medical paraphernalia, and by dint of their rather high build and upright lines ingress and egress were effected with comparative facility.

Victoria Coupe
The victoria coupe was a stretched three-quarter coupe incorporating four seats and larger quarter lights. The majority were fabricated with solid roofs, although folding hoods were optional.

Victoria Coupe *(US)*
The American victoria coupe was broadly similar in layout and general arrangement to the victoria coupe outlined above, with the exception that quarter lights were seldom fitted.

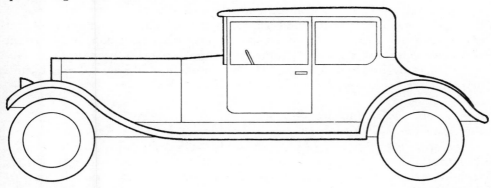

Victoria Coupe

Double Coupe
See Limousine section.

Coupelette
See Landaulette section.

Fixed-Head Coupe
A fixed-head coupe is simply a coupe with a fixed roof. The appellation covers all such coupe bodies irrespective of other more colourful titles

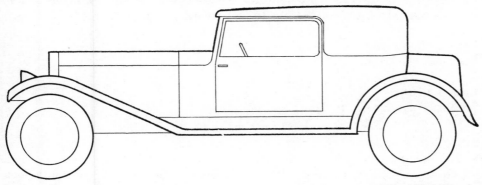

Fixed-Head Coupe   41

that may have been applied to them; thus a solid-roofed three-quarter coupe is equally a fixed-head coupe, as is, say, a solid-roofed sportsman's coupe. Nonetheless the appellation has been very widely utilised in its own right, the Jaguar XK150 Fixed-Head Coupe being a fairly modern example.

Coupe Limousine

The type of body normally associated with the word limousine is a large closed multi-seater, so that this title of coupe limousine appears at first glance to be something of a misnomer. In this context however, the limousine suffix merely indicates a commensurately spacious body; in fact a coupe limousine was a foursome fixed-head coupe, generally two-light with blind rear quarters and sufficiently capacious to maintain reasonable rear legroom although in practice the latter condition was not always fully met.

The designation was but rarely utilised, most bodies of this nature being referred to simply as coupes or fixed-head coupes.

Club Coupe *(US)*, Club Brougham *(US)*, Business Coupe *(US)*

These three solid-roofed American body styles resembled in all major respects the American victoria coupe, being two-door four-seater cars with or without quarter lights. All three terms were in quite common usage up to and beyond the Second World War.

Opera Coupe *(US)*

This American coupe was a somewhat larger foursome fixed-head coupe than the above bodies, indeed several of this breed were effectively two-door saloons. The opera coupe was chiefly designed in a rather formal style and was often elegantly accoutred.

Sport Coupe *(US)*, Sportsman Coupe *(US)*

Fairly common in the United States between the wars, these were two or four-seater fixed-head coupes of sleek, sporting appearance.

Faux Coupe

See Saloon section.

Gran Turismo

See under *Sports Car* in Tourer section.

Drop-Head Coupe

A drop-head coupe is by definition a coupe equipped with a folding hood. Infrequently employed nowadays as a body title, drop-head coupe was

adopted as a designation in its own right by coachbuilders and manufacturers during the late 1920s and early 1930s in lieu of older designations such as coupe cabriolet.

The definitive version of a drop-head coupe of both before and after World War II was a two-door, four-seater car complete with a snug, well-fitting folding hood and, on several post-war models, quarter lights behind the door windows to relieve the often sizable blind rear quarters; the 1938 LG6 Lagonda and 1950 Sunbeam Talbot 90 Drop-Head Coupes are representative of this frequently fleet and graceful style.

Two-seater open cars were but seldom called drop-head coupes, chiefly being termed roadsters or suchlike, whereas an occasional pre-war four-door drop-head model was referred to as a drop-head coupe, though incorrectly, since the layout of this body did not qualify it as a coupe of any form. According to English bodywork nomenclature a motor car of this nature was specifically a cabriolet (qv).

Drop-Head Coupe

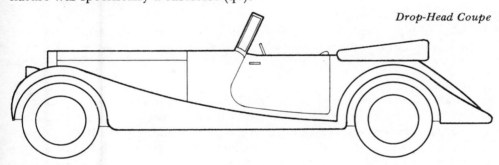

Convertible Coupe *(US)*

This is the American equivalent of the drop-head coupe; the designation is somewhat unusual in that it has been in constant usage for more than sixty-five years, a feat few other non horse-drawn carriage-type body titles can match. Unhappily though, in the past two or three years the range of convertible coupes available to American customers has been drastically reduced, for reasons connected with variously harsh safety regulations and ultimate product standardisation, to the point where Cadillac offered the last American convertible coupes for sale in April 1976.

Although this type of body has been fabricated in comparatively low numbers (by American standards) over the last decade, it always attracted a consistent and enthusiastic demand, so that its demise is doubly to be regretted.

The derivation of the term convertible coupe is self-evident: that is, a coupe readily convertible from the open to the closed state and vice versa. In line with the English drop-head coupe, it was restricted to two-door form only, though there were inevitable exceptions to this rule; in general, four-door versions were called *Convertible Sedans*.

43

Automobile body design

Convertible

Derived from the Transatlantic term convertible coupe, the convertible is the post-war equivalent of the drop-head coupe; nevertheless both these designations existed as alternatives until 1960 or thereabouts, after which time the drop-head coupe nomenclature was dropped in favour of convertible.

Very few convertibles are presently produced in this country and those that are are very expensive, and therefore exclusive, one case in point being the Rolls-Royce Corniche model. The days of the relatively cheap family convertible have gone forever.

There was an isolated instance of application of American terminology to an English drop-head body style, namely the Barker-bodied 3-litre Daimler Convertible Coupe introduced in 1953.

Decapotable, Decouvrable

Translated approximately as 'uncoverable', these are two relatively modern French appellations synonymous with drop-head coupe or convertible.

Cabriolet

Originally developed from the refined horse-drawn carriage of the same name, the cabriolet body has been designed and constructed in several forms since Edwardian times. Essentially, however, it was and remains the European equivalent to the drop-head coupe or convertible, in either two or four-seater guise. In the United Kingdom the term was utilised for drop-head bodies of this nature until the early 1930s, and thereafter as an occasional 'exotic' alternative to drop-head coupe, though in the main throughout the period 1910-1940 the standard coachbuilt English cabriolet per se was a four-door, four or six-light convertible body of generally large dimensions and formal lines.

Coupe Cabriolet *(US: Convertible Cabriolet)*

The coupe cabriolet was a two-door, two-seater or close-coupled four-seater coupe furnished with a folding hood. Extant from the Edwardian era until the end of the Vintage period, the coupe cabriolet was a highly-regarded form of bodywork; the title was by definition generic, embracing, for instance, drop-head forms of the victoria coupe, doctor's coupe and three-quarter coupe, all three therefore being classed as coupe cabriolets. The term was superseded by drop-head coupe between the late 1920s and the early 1930s.

Three-Quarter Coupe Cabriolet

See above and Three-Quarter Coupe.

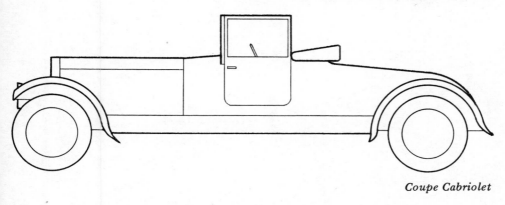

Coupe Cabriolet

Convertible Victoria *(US)*

The convertible victoria was a luxurious American two-light convertible coupe accommodating four people, analogous to the English drop-head coupe. A distinctive feature of most convertible victorias was the presence of extensive blind rear quarter panels as a consequence of the use of long bodies and thus large, heavy hoods. Alternatively, but only very occasionally called a *Convertible Victoria Coupe,* this type of body was almost always coachbuilt. Discontinued as a designation after World War II, one of the last of the line and to many eyes the most covetable, was the Howard Darrin-designed Packard Super Eight Convertible Victoria of 1939-41.

Saloon Coupe Cabriolet

This resounding title was especially contrived for a mid-1930s Hooper-bodied close-coupled two-door saloon whose solid roof had been supplanted by a full-length collapsible hood - which is another description of a drop-head coupe.

Drop-Head Sedanca Coupe

The drop-head sedanca coupe was a straightforward drop-head coupe furnished with a three-position hood (qv), of which the Rolls-Royce Phantom II Continental with such coachwork by Gurney Nutting serves as a magnificent example. In general these bodies were simply referred to as drop-head coupes.

45

Automobile body design

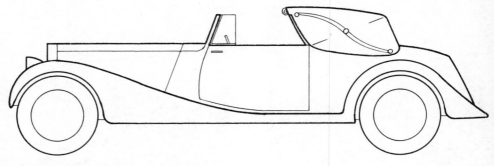

Drop-Head Sedanca Coupe

Coupe de Ville, Sedanca Coupe

Both styles were by definition identical, ie a sedanca coupe was a coupe de ville and vice versa, but in practice a sedanca coupe was generally a fixed-head de ville version of the straightforward drop-head coupe (or more correctly the drop-head sedanca coupe), whereas the term coupe de ville was very frequently applied to a close-coupled sedanca de ville body (qv).

Coupes de ville were popular amongst the concours d'elegance set between the wars, and some superb examples were realised. The largest and most impressive coupes de ville were undoubtedly the 'Coupe Napoleon' constructed by Binder of Paris for Ettore Bugatti and mounted on his personal 1927 Type 41 Bugatti Royale chassis, together with a similar but slightly modified version on a later Royale chassis.

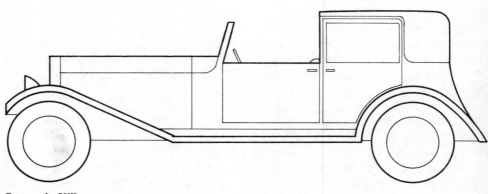

Coupe de Ville

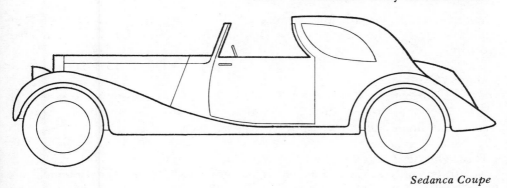

Sedanca Coupe

Sports Sedanca Coupe

An exceedingly rare but evocative body, the sports sedanca coupe was a sedanca coupe of deliberately swept lines exhibiting a considerable degree of sporting appeal and panache.

Panel Brougham *(US)*

The American panel brougham was analogous to the British and European coupe de ville; it was of formal appearance and frequently incorporated razor-edged lines to the rear compartment.

CABRIOLET

Cabriolet

As already intimated under *Cabriolet* in the coupe section, the cabriolet to European eyes is a convertible of any size or layout, from the relatively small roadster-style Porsche 356 of the 1950s and early 1960s to the very large and heavy four-door Mercedes-Benz 300B of around 1953. To a Briton of pre-World War II days a cabriolet generally summoned up a picture of a coachbuilt four-door, four or six-light drop-head body that was sufficiently sizable to carry at least four people in comfort. It is the English-style of cabriolet to which this section is devoted.

Most cabriolets built between the wars were effectively refined tourers, in that they combined the general arrangement of touring bodies with a higher level of weather protection; winding or lifting glass door and side windows whose frames and cant rails either folded away with the hood or hinged down flush with the body sides when the hood was collapsed were de rigueur, and divisions were optional (normally standard fitments on de ville versions) since cabriolets were often purchased for formal usage.

Cabriolet was a generic title in the same manner as tourer and coupe, so that any variations of this body type - including all those

47

Automobile body design

hereunder - could be correctly termed cabriolets alone, without qualification. This observation does not hold good for the fixed-head versions, however.

Single Cabriolet
Single cabriolet was the strictly precise designation given to a four-light cabriolet, although the designation was seldom employed outside coachbuilding establishments.

Three-Quarter Cabriolet
Not to be confused with the *Three-Quarter Coupe Cabriolet* body which was also occasionally called a three-quarter cabriolet, this title was similar to the single cabriolet in that it was a definitive designation, in this case applied to a six-light cabriolet and was often used as a title both within and without the motor trade till well into the 1930s.

All-Weather Cabriolet, Convertible Cabriolet *(US: Convertible Sedan, Convertible Berline, All-Weather Phaeton, Convertible Phaeton, Phaeton Sedan, Convertible Phaeton Sedan)*
Both these cabriolets were identical in principle to and often virtually indistinguishable from the all-weather tourer (qv) of the Edwardian and Vintage eras. Convertible cabriolet was a rather later, mid-1920s term that co-existed with the all-weather cabriolet appellation until the turn of the 1930s, when the latter fell into disuse.

Divisions were rarely to be found in convertible cabriolets and never fitted to all-weather cabriolets.

Torpedo Cabriolet *(US: Speedster Phaeton)*
The torpedo cabriolet was a four or six-light cabriolet body designed on the flush-sided torpedo tourer (qv) principle, in conjunction with sleek semi-sporting lines.

Saloon Cabriolet
A speciality of the renowned English coachbuilders Salmons of Newport Pagnell, the saloon cabriolet was a four-door, four or six-light drop-head body in which the window frames and cant rails were permanently fixed in position, akin to a saloon body; its resemblance to the latter was most evident when the hood was erected, and hence the designation.

Fixed Cabriolet, Fixed-Head Cabriolet, Faux Cabriolet
These were three titles for a body that superficially resembled a straightforward cabriolet and was similar in layout and appointments to the

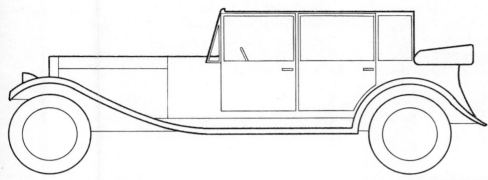

Saloon Cabriolet

latter, the distinction being that a solid roof was furnished in lieu of the familiar folding hood. The roof was in many instances covered in leather or suchlike material and the rear quarter panels garnished with dummy landau irons in order to simulate the appearance of a folding hood: *Faux* is the French word for 'false' and therefore pertinent in this particular context. A division, with or without a de ville front, was occasionally specified.

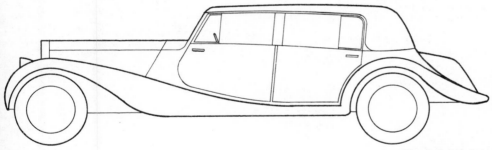

Fixed Cabriolet

Cabriolet *(US)*

To add to the wide dissimilarity surrounding English and European forms of cabriolet, the term as used in the United States pertained to a fixed-head cabriolet with an open drive or de ville front compartment as standard. More precisely, the open drive version, with folding or detachable front roof and side curtains, was the definitive American cabriolet whereas the de ville configuration, in which glass windows were substituted for side curtains in the pursuit of improved weather protection, was known as an *All-Weather Cabriolet* (not to be confused with the English style of the same name). Alternative terms for the latter were *Town* or *Stationary Cabriolet*.

The closest equivalents to the conventional folding-hood English cabriolet, but still containing open drive or de ville format, were the *Convertible Town, Full-Collapsible* and *Transformable Cabriolets*.   49

Automobile body design

A confusing situation, but as a 'rule of thumb' the Transatlantic cabriolet per se always featured a solid-roofed rear compartment in the manner of a sedanca de ville (qv), unless accompanied by such qualifications as transformable, convertible or full-collapsible, which denoted the provision of a fully-folding rear compartment hood.

Sport Cabriolet *(US)*
The American sport cabriolet was a rakishly-lined town cabriolet (see above).

Cabriolet de Ville,
Cabriolet Sedanca de Ville, Double Cabriolet
The cabriolet de ville was an archetypal cabriolet of either four-light or six-light formation which was equipped with a modified fully-collapsible hood: when this hood was in the closed position the portion over the front seats could be furled to produce a de ville status - a three-position hood in effect. The majority of cabriolets de ville were commissioned and purchased for formal usage, and therefore divisions were included in the generally very comprehensive specifications. *Cabriolet Sedanca de Ville* and *Double Cabriolet* are alternative designations for a cabriolet de ville body.

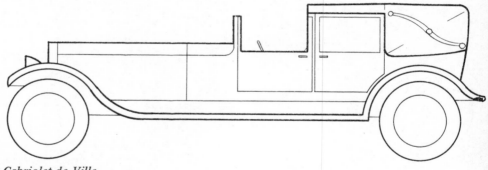

Cabriolet de Ville

Three-Quarter Cabriolet de Ville
In the same way that a three-quarter cabriolet was interpreted as a six-light model, the three-quarter cabriolet de ville was the six-light variation of the cabriolet de ville style.

Salamanca, Salamanca Cabriolet
Originally designed just prior to the First World War by the Spanish nobleman and Rolls-Royce agent, Count Carlos de Salamanca, the salamanca (or salamanca cabriolet) was a four-light formal cabriolet de ville mounted exclusively on Rolls-Royce chassis. Interiors were noted for their sumptuous appointments, and occasional seats were provided to increase the carrying capacity when necessary.

The salamanca was built in some numbers during the 1920s, and replicas by the American coachbuilders Brewster were constructed on the New England-built Springfield Rolls-Royce Silver Ghost and Phantom I chassis; called Special Salamancas, these Transatlantic versions were offered with a rigid roof to the rear compartment as an alternative arrangement to the more usual folding hood, a conversion which brought this style into line with the conventional American cabriolet (qv).

SALOON

Saloon

During the First World War wide-ranging and rapid progress had been made in the fields of metallurgical knowledge and mass-production expertise, made necessary by the incessant needs and demands of the fighting forces, so that it was natural that these techniques were put to use in the years immediately following cessation of hostilities in 1918; the consequence of application of mass-production in the motor industry - following not only those methods learnt in wartime but also the pioneering work of Henry Ford in the United States before the war - was the introduction of the comparatively cheap all-metal saloon car, destined for a vast new market comprising the broad mass of the population in this country that hitherto could not have afforded such luxuries as motor cars. The saloon increasingly overtook the tourer in popularity, until by the 1930s it was by far and away paramount over all other body styles combined. It has remained so ever since.

The saloon is fundamentally a four or six-light closed car with seating space for four or more people; two, or more commonly four, doors are provided, together with winding, lifting or sliding glass door windows. Side windows are either permanently fixed, or hinged for purposes of ventilation. Depending as always on the cost of the car, interior appointments differ greatly, from the very basic 2CV Citroen to the opulent Rolls-Royce Camargue at something over twenty times the cost, though a variety of fixtures and fittings have enjoyed a national vogue at one period or another, a notable instance being the sunshine roof which was common to virtually all saloons up to the Second World War and which is undergoing a resurgence of popularity today.

Since the saloon has always been specifically geared to the owner-driver and intended as family transport, a division was and is a most unusual fitment; indeed the insertion of same would prove an exceptionally difficult task in most modern saloons, since the space given over to rear legroom is already considerably restricted - certainly very much more so than in their pre-war forebears.

Automobile body design

Saloon

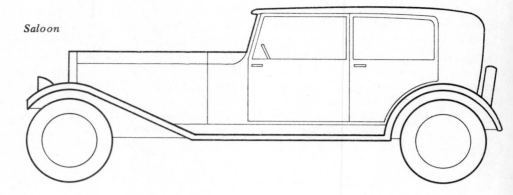

Sedan *(US)*
Originally a hand-cart used in the township of Sedan in France for transport of fish, and then a single-seat conveyance carried by two bearers (the sedan chair), the sedan is the Transatlantic counterpart of the saloon and corresponds in general arrangement to the latter, although it is usually of greater size and engine capacity.

Double Saloon
See Limousine section.

Berline
Evolved from a form of horse-drawn coach (the Berlin), the berline is the general European term for a saloon.

Berlina
The Berlina is a saloon in Italian bodywork nomenclature; it is derived from the same source as berline.

Double Berline
See Limousine section.

Berline de Voyage
The French equivalent of the touring saloon (qv). 'De voyage' may also be found attached to 'double berline' or 'limousine' and simply indicates touring versions of those styles.

Conduite Interieure
Translating literally as 'Interior Drive', the conduite interieure is widely used in French-speaking countries as a generic term for all saloon or saloon-type bodies.

Coach

Coach was a term occasionally employed by a number of French motor manufacturers to denote a car supplied with a foursome two-door saloon body; the Hotchkiss Anjou Coach and Bugatti Type 57 Ventoux Coach are two examples of the usage of this appellation.

Coach *(US)*

Initially a variety of open four-seater car of the Veteran era, many American manufacturers and coachbuilders applied the term coach to two-door sedan designs from the late Edwardian age up till the mid-1930s. Four-door sedans were but very rarely called coaches, and those that were were of pre-1917 vintage.

Fabric Saloon, Weymann Saloon

A fabric saloon was a saloon the bodywork of which comprised an ash frame panelled in fabric. Though very frequently utilised on open tourers of the Vintage period this form of construction did not readily lend itself to saloon bodies: its inherent lack of rigidity coupled with the flexible chassis of the time was reasonably tolerable in an open car, but a closed body necessitated a considerable degree of torsional stiffness in order to counteract the chassis flexibility and that the fabric-panelled body could not properly provide. This consequently led to problems of distortion of, for instance, door frames, a critical factor in a closed body, and a gradual disintegration of the framework through vibration. Nevertheless, the attraction of this method of construction was its lightness compared with metal-panelled bodies.

    A Frenchman, M. Weymann, patented a development of the ash-framed, fabric-panelled body during the mid-1920s which transformed the distortion and wear characteristics. Weymann bodies were built under licence in several countries, including the United Kingdom, and were deservedly popular - though time has shown that they were not as durable as sheet-steel and aluminium-panelled bodies.

Pillarless Saloon

Notwithstanding its unconventional structure, the pillarless saloon vaunted a number of adherents amongst the British and Continental motor manufacturing and coachbuilding industries from the 1930s until 1960 or thereabouts. Externally a straightforward four-door saloon whose doors closed towards each other as viewed on either side, ie the front door was hinged about its forward edge and the corresponding rear door rear-hinged, the body was constructed without a central shut pillar, so that the area presented by the open doors was unobstructed by framework - a factor that considerably facilitated ingress and egress. The well-loved Lancia Aprilia of the late 1930s and mid-1940s was such a saloon, as indeed were several subsequent Lancia models.

53

Automobile body design

The term pillarless may also be applied to a saloon, or indeed any other closed body style, in which the rear quarter light on either side of the body was inserted without a vertical frame pillar at its leading edge and the adjacent door window was correspondingly unframed at its trailing edge, resulting in an expanse of glass equal to the area of the two windows which was undivided by metalwork. In the interests of weatherproofing the quarter lights were inset inboard of and slightly overlapped the door lights. Several models of Sunbeam and Sunbeam-Talbot cars made between 1936 and 1954 contained this particular window treatment, being the most familiar examples of this type of saloon.

Touring Saloon *(US: Touring Sedan)*

The vast majority of saloons built before World War II suffered from a lamentable lack of accommodation for more than an exceedingly modest amount of luggage: saloons of the Vintage era and early 1930s either made no provision for luggage at all or relied on folding grids at the rear - in both cases a roof rack had to be used for occasions such as family holidays, or the luggage was sent ahead by train. Later saloons contained small enclosed boots housing the spare wheel which occupied a large percentage of the available space; however, stout bootlids which opened down to a horizontal position permitted the carriage of several suitcases or a trunk.

A touring saloon was a saloon whose conspicuous feature was a large boot of sufficient capacity to accept the amount of baggage necessary for long-distance touring. The term was sometimes utilised in the first decade after the Second World War for coachbuilt touring limousines (qv) without divisions; with the advent of amply-booted post-war saloons the designation became defunct in general usage.

Sports Saloon, Sporting Saloon, *(US: Sport Sedan)* Sportsman's Saloon

These were four-door, generally four-light saloons, often rather more close-coupled and having slightly lower rooflines than the conventional saloon style. Current from the late 1920s to the outbreak of war in 1939 and held in high esteem throughout this period, all three bodies differed principally from their more common brethren in possessing enclosed boots of reasonable size.

Sports Saloon Limousine

This was a somewhat pretentious title for a sports saloon fitted with a division, an exceedingly rare combination.

Salonette

Salonette was an appellation devised and employed exclusively by the MG Car Company in the 1930s for a sports saloon product.

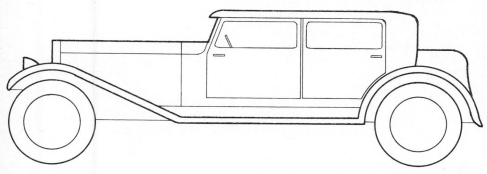

Sportsman's Saloon

Streamline Saloon
In vogue during the mid-1930s, the streamline saloon style exhibited sleek, curvaceous lines combined with a strong horizontal emphasis; the roof contours merged succinctly into the back panel and swept down to bumper level in a gentle slope - a forerunner of what is in modern parlance a *Fastback.*

Coachbuilt streamline saloons were almost entirely of two-door, four-light configuration, whereas those manufacturers who mass-produced streamline saloons tended to favour four-door, six-light bodies. The latter were but pale shadows of the exuberant, sensuously-shaped streamline saloons created by numerous coachbuilding concerns.

Town Sedan *(US),* **Formal Sedan** *(US)*
The town or formal sedan was a sedan of sober and restrained lines that was deliberately designed to exude a formal mien, though it was not necessarily utilised for that purpose.

Club Sedan *(US)*
This was a four-door sedan of conservative conception that incorporated generously-rounded edges and corners to the roof, wings and back panel.

Saloon Coupe,
Close-Coupled Saloon, Short-Coupled Saloon *(US: Sedanette)*
These three terms were applied to a close-coupled, two-door, four-light saloon. Especially favoured by coachbuilders, the more exotic term *Saloon Coupe* is most apt in that the body type corresponds to a 'cut' (coupe) or 'short' saloon, and then again it could also be regarded as a fixed-head coupe; thus the two terms saloon and coupe in juxtaposition effect an admirably precise designation. Some magnificent examples of saloon coupe bodywork were mounted on Rolls-Royce Wraith and Silver Dawn chassis by Messrs Hooper just before and shortly after the Second World War.

Automobile body design

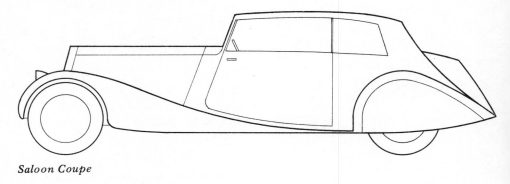

Saloon Coupe

Berlinette
Literally 'small berline', berlinette is the French equivalent term for a close-coupled saloon or saloon coupe.

Berlinetta
This is the equivalent Italian term for a close-coupled saloon or saloon coupe. In the last two decades the term has come to be increasingly associated with two-seater or occasional four-seater Ferrari Gran Turismo (and sports-racing) cars fabricated by such illustrious Carrozzeria as Vignale, Bertone and Pininfarina.

Faux Coupe
The faux ('false') coupe was a designation employed but rarely by a few French coachbuilders to signify a saloon coupe, usually of comparatively light weight. Such a car was an individually-bodied Lago-Talbot Faux Coupe of 1950 vintage.

Hardtop, Hardtop Saloon *(US: Hardtop Sedan)*
A body that combines some of the benefits of an open car with all those of a saloon, the hardtop originated in the United States during the 1940s. It is a two or four-door saloon featuring pillarless side and door windows whose frames are attached to and move vertically with them; all these windows are capable of being fully retracted into the doors and side panels to create an entirely open area from windscreen to rear quarter panel on either side of the car. Although the roof is non-collapsible a practical semblance of open motoring can thus be achieved with ease and simplicity.

      The hardtop has a worldwide following, and is especially popular in countries of equable climate. The best-known British car of this type is the Sunbeam Rapier, which was manufactured by the Rootes Group in three successive designs since 1955.

Sedanca de Ville *(US: Town Car)*

Extant from the commencement of the Vintage era right through till the mid-1960s, the sedanca de ville was a body style of high status and surpassing elegance constructed on a variety of chassis of greater or lesser length and refinement; as a rule the larger the chassis the better the visual proportions of the body, so that those sedancas de ville using such bases as Rolls-Royce and Hispano-Suiza chassis were almost invariably most impressive in both size and appearance. The majority of British, European and American coachbuilders fabricated sedancas de ville at one time or another; the British coachbuilding industry proved pre-eminent in output and quality of design of these bodies.

A sedanca de ville ('Sedanca' was coined by the Spanish Count Salamanca, in the very early 1920s) was a closed four-door, generally four-light car of large-saloon or limousine proportions which was equipped with a division and de ville front. Occasional seats were customarily but by no means compulsorily supplied and the quality - and quantity - of interior fixtures and appointments bore witness both to the high cost of the bodywork and the formal use for which the car was intended. Few owners however went to the lengths of one wealthy gentleman who commissioned Aubusson brocade seats, gilt fixtures and baroque painted panels, all in the Louis Quatorze style, for the rear compartment of his Phantom I Rolls-Royce Sedanca de Ville.

So many exemplary designs were created throughout the forty-year history of this body style that to cite one above all others would be rather unjust; perhaps the most equable compromise is to quote as an example the very last sedanca de ville design of all, the James Young-bodied Rolls-Royce Phantom V Sedanca de Ville the final commission for which was completed in 1965 *(see Part 3, Figure 16)*.

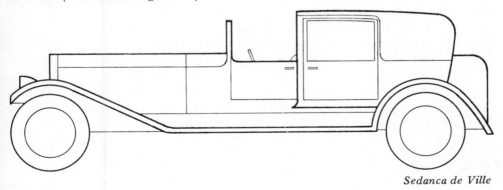

Sedanca de Ville

Berline de Ville

Utilised during the 1920s and especially the 1930s, berline de ville was the French nomenclature for a sedanca de ville body style.

Automobile body design

LIMOUSINE

Limousine *(US: Limousine, Imperial Limousine, Berline)*
The archetypal formal car, the limousine arose during the early Edwardian era, was produced in significant numbers and reached its zenith of design during the twenty years between the World Wars, and is still manufactured today, albeit in small quantities. The word limousine is related to the French township of Limousin, whose claim to fame was the loan of its name to a form of protective broad-cloth used for outer garments in the eighteenth and nineteenth centuries; the properties of Limousine cloth led to its eventual usage for carriage hoods, so that when the horseless carriage epoch dawned the word was gradually transformed in meaning to become associated with large, heavy closed cars.

As already explained in the Features and Fitments section the overall percentage of limousines - and other formal bodies - constructed before, and for many years after the First World War were of open drive configuration; enclosed drive limousines became de rigueur from the late 1920s onwards though occasional usage was made thereafter of open drive, more particularly in warmer climates than Britain and Northern Europe.

The limousine was, and remains, a large four-door, four or six-light closed car incorporating a division in conjunction with two or three occasional seats situated in the rear compartment. Not necessarily mounted on the largest available chassis of any period, bodies were marked, as were all formal body types, by differences in appointment between front and rear compartment. Maintaining as he did a chauffeur to drive the limousine - sometimes accompanied by a footman for the sake of appearance, depending on his wealth and sense of ostentation - the owner expected, and generally received, a higher degree of comfort in the rear compartment.

Of the very limited number of limousines available nowadays the majority are based upon suitable saloons lengthened by insertion of a section behind the front doors, thereby creating the amount of legroom desirable in a limousine body together with sufficient space for a division and occasional seats. Two such limousines are those fashioned on the English Ford Granada Saloon and American Lincoln Continental Sedan by Messrs Coleman-Milne and Lehmann-Peterson respectively.

To the German motor industry however, the word limousine has contrasting connotations to the more normally accepted application of the term: limousine is utilised as the generic designation for the saloon body style, irrespective of size, number of doors or degree of 'formality'. Thus, to a German, a limousine can denote anything from the tiny two-door Lloyd of the 1950s to the vast six-door flagship of the Mercedes-Benz fleet - coincidentally both share the model designation '600'.

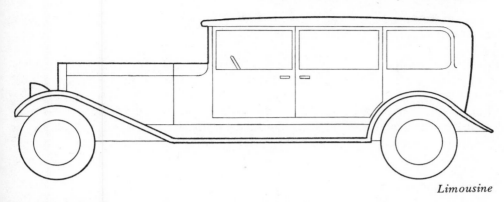

Limousine

Town Carriage
A throwback to the days before the invention of the internal combustion engine, this was a designation used at times by coachbuilders prior to World War I as an alternative to limousine.

Town Limousine
An appellation which could be justly applied to most limousines of any period, town limousine was pertinent to a pre-1914 limousine whose open drive characteristic had been taken to its logical conclusion: sans roof, windscreen or doors.

Saloon Limousine
A style which gained a certain measure of acceptance during the harsh years of the 1930s, though a few examples had been manufactured in the previous two decades, the saloon limousine was a limousine built without a division and therefore aimed specifically at the owner-driver.

Sports Saloon Limousine
See Saloon section.

Double Saloon
This was a seldom-used alternative designation for an early saloon limousine.

Double Berline
The double berline was a rare pre-First World War limousine or saloon limousine featuring compartments formed individually in horse-drawn coach style, so that it resembled twin coaches (Berlins) locked together in tandem.

Double Coupe
This was an even rarer, smaller version of the Edwardian double berline, fabricated without a division.

Automobile body design

Coupe Limousine
See Coupe section.

Sedan Limousine *(US)*
The sedan limousine found during the 1920s and 1930s in the United States came in two forms, as a limousine without a division or as a dual-purpose limousine - ie adaptable for the owner-driver in addition to formal, chauffeur-driven usage - that included a division so designed to be as inconspicuous as possible when retracted. The latter type of sedan limousine was a speciality of the American coachbuilders LeBaron.

Touring Limousine
Arising in the 1930s, the touring limousine was analogous to the touring saloon (qv) in that it provided a commodious enclosed boot to meet the demands of extended touring, though unlike its saloon cousin the limousine version was intended to be driven by a chauffeur and therefore a division was supplied as a standard fitting.

A touring limousine often differed from more orthodox limousines in being a degree more close-coupled (to allow room for the large boot) and having less conservative, more flamboyant lines suited to its touring role.

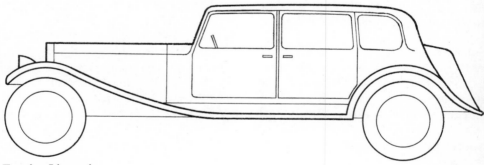

Touring Limousine

Sports Limousine *(US: Sport Limousine)*
A form constructed by few coachbuilders and therefore a very rare type, the sports limousine was a touring or saloon limousine of unusually sleek, even rakish lines. Because of the length and height characteristics concomitant upon limousine bodies a cohesive and balanced sports limousine design was difficult to achieve, and - bar one or two exceptions - some peculiar shapes resulted.

Brougham, Brougham Limousine
Derived from the well-regarded horse-drawn brougham coach of the nineteenth century (named after its progenitor, Lord Brougham), the

brougham or brougham limousine was a formal four-light open drive limousine body of distinctly carriage-like aspect, particularly in respect of the rear compartment which was in addition almost invariably razor-edged, though a number of broughams were in fact constructed with more subtly-rounded features.

The brougham was often a rather shorter body than a conventional limousine, and existed as a motor car style for more than forty years until the outbreak of World War II. Strictly speaking this body was definitively a *Single Brougham* though the full term was not utilised.

Double Brougham

An open drive limousine in the same mould as a (single) brougham, the double brougham was fabricated with a larger rear compartment in order to increase the available legroom and/or to accommodate occasional rear seats. The enlargement was generally effected by incorporation of a D-front.

A very much rarer style than its smaller relation, the double brougham went out of fashion at the end of the Edwardian era.

Limousine de Ville

A limousine de ville was simply an orthodox limousine furnished with a de ville front compartment; unlike the sedanca de ville whose size and overall layout it resembled, this body was of six-light formation as standard. A limousine de ville body also frequently exhibited ultra-conservative lines which in combination with its large dimensions gave it a massively imposing presence.

Since World War II those limousines constructed with a de ville front were called sedancas de ville as opposed to limousines de ville, whether of four or six-light configuration: the reason behind this change in designation is not clear, but it may be that the term sedanca de ville was more esoteric and therefore commanded more interest.

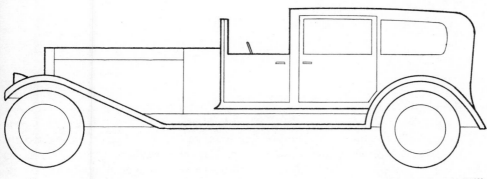

Limousine de Ville   61

Automobile body design

Coupe Limousine de Ville
A thoroughly confusing appellation in that it bore no relation whatsoever to either a coupe or a coupe limousine and therefore was technically a misnomer of the first magnitude, coupe limousine de ville was applied, so far as is known, by only one coachbuilder, the Paris firm of Binder, to a six-light limousine de ville body distinguished by an abnormally low roofline.

Town Car *(US)*, Town Brougham *(US)*
The designation town car was the Transatlantic equivalent of sedanca de ville or limousine de ville. The term also applied to a limousine featuring a form of open drive where the front compartment was entirely devoid of a roof.

The town brougham was a similar but often larger form of bodywork to the English brougham, in either open drive or de ville format.

Brougham de Ville,
Brougham Limousine de Ville
The brougham de ville, or brougham limousine de ville, was the later form of brougham, built from the late 1920s till 1939, in which the open drive configuration was replaced by a de ville front.

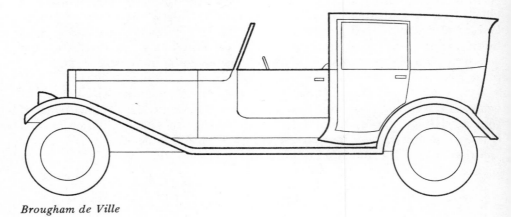

Brougham de Ville

LANDAULETTE

Landaulette *(US: Touring Cabriolet)*
The ultimate in formal bodies, the landaulette (or landaulet) was a progressive development of the horsedrawn landau as adapted to the motor car chassis. A landau was a carriage in which the passengers rode vis-a-vis, ie the two rows of seats faced each other, access to which was gained via central doors on either side of the body; fore and aft hoods were provided,

each of which folded down behind the corresponding row of seats, and when raised were locked together transversely above the doors. The addition of 'ette' (in this instance 'lette') to a suitable word form in the French language produces a diminutive of the original word, so that a 'landaulette' is a small or half-landau; extrapolating therefrom a landaulette should comprise half the characteristics of its parent, ie a single folding hood over a single row of seats. Which in practice it does.

In sum therefore, a landaulette is a limousine or large saloon with division in which the portion of the roof over the rear seat is capable of being collapsed, thus exposing the rear seat to the open air. Built in surprisingly large numbers from the Veteran era until 1914, and thereafter in steadily decreasing quantities, the landaulette was, and still is, employed for such occasions as State ceremonies, where the essence of the occasion is to enable the sovereign, member of royalty, head of state and suchlike personages to be seen by their subjects. Not only is the landaulette an ideal car for this purpose but also the relatively small hood can be raised with facility in the event of unforeseen eventualities such as sudden inclement weather, a factor that tells against the usage of a cabriolet-type car whose large cumbersome hood can take a considerable span of time to erect.

The landaulette was heavily favoured by the nobility and gentry in the Edwardian era; in those days class distinction was absolute, so that an aristocrat or privileged citizen felt it incumbent upon himself to 'show himself' to the populace at large, to which role the landaulette again lent itself admirably.

In this day and age only a handful of landaulettes are fabricated annually, chiefly adaptations of the Mercedes-Benz 600 Pullman and Daimler Limousines, plus the very occasional one-off body; an instance of the latter is the Rolls-Royce Phantom VI Special Landaulette by Mulliner-Park Ward, displayed at the 1974 London Motor Show.

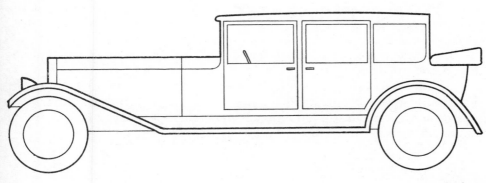

Landaulette   63

Automobile body design

Three-Quarter Landaulette
This was the epithet given to an open drive landaulette of six-light construction where only the front door windows were absent; this aspect of open drive was frequently utilised from the late Edwardian period thenceforward on many types of formal bodywork since it rendered a more reasonable degree of comfort for the chauffeur than did the windscreen-less or roof-less variety of open drive configuration.

The equivalent six-light enclosed drive landaulette was similarly called an *Enclosed Three-Quarter Landaulette.* Both designations were current until enclosed drive became the orthodox configuration on formal coachwork during the late 1920s, the resulting bodywork thereafter being termed simply *Landaulette.*

Single Landaulette - Pre-World War I
The early version of the single landaulette body type constructed from around 1900 until 1914 was an open drive body in which the entire roof aft of the division could be folded. The two-light rear compartment was normally furnished with removable window frames, or frames that hinged down to lie flush with the body sides when the hood was collapsed. The glass division, which could be had in retractable form though more often it was permanently fixed in place, was part of a permanent partition between the compartments that was built to the height of the raised hood. The front compartment was roof-less, so that in open form the car closely resembled the later cabriolet de ville, apart from the upstanding division and its corresponding frame.

Single Landaulette (1)
There were two kinds of post-Great War body to which the term single landaulette applied, the very much more well-known of which is described under *Coupelette* (qv); for the sake of continuity that single landaulette which most closely resembled its Edwardian forerunner is described at this juncture. Just to complicate matters this particular single landaulette coachwork was also known as a *Saloon Landaulette* (qv); for most purposes the body was more commonly referred to as either the latter or simply by the generic title landaulette.

The body was of identical layout to its earlier counterpart, except that a rigid roof was provided for the front compartment and the division was generally capable of retraction, comparable to other forms of formal bodywork.

Single Landaulette (2)
See Coupelette.

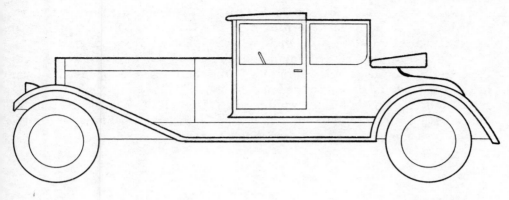

Single Landaulette

Double Landaulette - Pre-World War I
The double landaulette of the Edwardian period was an open drive body with a two-light rear compartment. A solid roof was fitted both to the front compartment and over the doors of the rear compartment, the remainder of the roof aft of the rear doors being of collapsible construction.

Double Landaulette
During the early 1920s a double landaulette was an open drive body complete with a two-light rear compartment and a division that differed from the single (or saloon) landaulette in the same manner that a double brougham differed from a single brougham, ie the rear compartment of the double landaulette was enlarged over that of the single landaulette by the incorporation of a D-front. In later years the double landaulette appellation was employed as a euphemism for the straightforward landaulette.

Limousine Landaulette - Pre-World War I
The pre-First World War limousine landaulette was very similar to the double landaulette of the same era except for the addition of rear quarter lights, over which the rigid section of the roof was extended.

Limousine Landaulette *(US: Berline Landaulette)*
The limousine landaulette of the Vintage years and the 1930s was a six-light enclosed drive landaulette; the designation was chiefly reserved for bodies of impressive size and appearance.

Saloon Landaulette *(US: Sedan Landaulette)*
Saloon landaulette was an epithet appended to two variations of landaulette coachwork; firstly to a conventional landaulette fabricated without a

Automobile body design

division, and secondly to a landaulette of open or enclosed drive, four or six-light format in which the roof over the front compartment was rigid whilst the entire roof aft of the division was capable of being collapsed.

The former type of saloon landaulette was but rarely built, whereas the latter was quite familiar during the 1920s and 1930s; in open drive form it was also known as a *Single Landaulette* (qv).

The previously-quoted Mulliner-Park Ward Rolls-Royce Phantom VI Special Landaulette, exhibited at the 1974 London Motor Show, is strictly speaking a saloon landaulette of the second style.

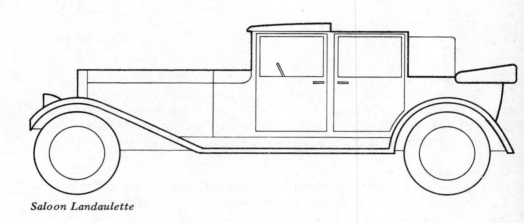

Saloon Landaulette

Coupelette

Contracted from *Coupe Landaulette,* ie a short-bodied landaulette, and extant during the Vintage era, the coupelette was a close-coupled foursome body of two-door, four-light configuration, similar to the *Victoria Coupe* (qv) in appearance, in which the roof over the front row of seats (ie over the door apertures) was solid whilst the remainder could be folded. A rather attractive body, especially when mounted on such medium-sized chassis as the Rolls-Royce Twenty, this form of landaulette coachwork was chiefly referred to and far more widely recognised as a *Single Landaulette*.

Coupelet *(US)*, Coupe Landaulette *(US)*

The coupelet, or coupe landaulette, was an American design of the same era and specification as the coupelette/single landaulette, with the exception that the rear quarter lights were omitted. This body was very much less frequently constructed in the United States than its British counterpart, which itself was coachwork of some rarity.

66

Landaulette de Ville,
Sedancalette de Ville *(US: Landaulette, All-Weather Landaulette)*
A uniquely adaptable form of landaulette design, the landaulette de ville or sedancalette *(Sedanca Landaulette)* de ville was a large six-light body that combined the dominant features of a sedanca de ville and landaulette, ie a de ville front in conjunction with a collapsible hood aft of the rear doors. The only permanently fixed portion of the roof was that section over the rear doors, to which a roof rack was often attached to supplement the conventional folding grid or moulded trunk (separated from the body) at the rear, since landaulette de ville-bodied cars were frequently utilised for long-distance touring in addition to formal usage.

Mainly constructed in the brief period around the late 1920s and early 1930s, the very expensive landaulette de ville bodies were mounted as a rule on lengthy chassis of the Hispano-Suiza and Isotta Fraschini variety.

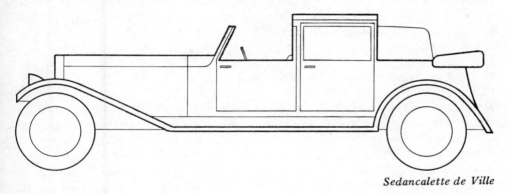

Sedancalette de Ville

ESTATE CAR

Wagonette, Brake, Shooting Brake (1)
A body type that stemmed from the horse-drawn carriage days, the wagonette, brake or shooting brake was a large vehicle providing basic accommodation for at least six people in a rear compartment in which the seats were ranged in rows along each side of the body, the occupants thus sitting sideways to the motion of the vehicle. Both fully-open and fully-closed bodies were built throughout the Veteran, Edwardian and Vintage periods, in addition to which combination bodies, in which the driving compartment was open and the rear closed, conversely the front closed or hooded with an open rear compartment, enjoyed a certain measure of demand. Entry was almost invariably via a door let into the back panel; side doors were not popular since their apertures detracted from the available seating space.

67

Automobile body design

Wagonette

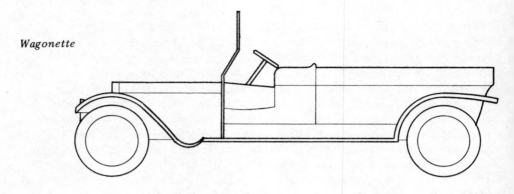

      All identical in general arrangement, the wagonette and brake were employed for such duties as conveyance of household staff or house guests, whilst a shooting brake catered for hunting parties and their equipment, being outfitted with gun racks, storage lockers and other pertinent appointments.

Estate Car, Station Wagon, Shooting Brake (2)
(US: Station Wagon, Estate Wagon)
Developed in the United States during the mid-1920s and gradually thereafter superseding the older styles in other countries the estate car, station wagon or shooting brake body placed more emphasis on carriage of bulky loads than transport of as many people as possible within a given space. The old title of *Shooting Brake* still survives, although not in its original context, and the later title of *Estate Car* has connotations of usage limited to large properties which is again no longer correct. Before the Sécond World War most British estate car bodies were handbuilt from scratch or adapted by coachbuilders from suitable saloons, whereas after the

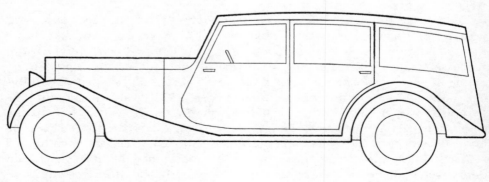

    Shooting Brake

cessation of hostilities in 1945 most manufacturers began to list estate cars which were mass-produced alongside, and furnished to the same levels of comfort as, saloons; in the last decade estate cars have mushroomed in popularity throughout Britain and the rest of Europe.

A closed two-door four-light or four-door six-light body, the estate car features somewhat van-like rear lines in conjunction with a door in the back panel for access to the load space; the latter can be augmented by folding down the rear seat back, thus reducing the seating capacity but enhancing the load-bearing facility. Several French (and American) estate cars are equipped with extra seats mounted in the extreme rear of the body, aimed at those customers who prize seating capacity over load space. Well-known examples of this modified style are the Peugeot 404 and 504 Familiale models.

By definition a car designed to convey personnel and baggage to and from railway stations, the station wagon was and is the American equivalent to the estate car; the term has, however, become increasingly utilised in this country as well.

Sports Estate Car

The *Sports* or *Sporting Estate Car* is a modern body style in which an estate rear is grafted onto a sports coupe of gran turismo design and is constructed with all the attendant estate car fittings such as folding rear seats and lift-up tailgate. The drawback to this particular species of dual-purpose bodywork is the restricted load volume, due chiefly to the inherently low roofline of its sports coupe progenitor, and therefore in absolute terms its utility is limited. Nonetheless the sports estate car does offer two seemingly incompatible body styles in successful combination and has attained an enthusiastic following amongst those motorists whose primary consideration is a motor car of some elan but who require greater than average carrying capacity.

Several varieties are or have lately been marketed, the most notable - and the originator of the series (apart from a few handbuilt Aston Martin DB4 Estate Cars of the early 1960s) - being the highly successful Reliant Scimitar GTE, derived from the earlier Scimitar GT (coupe) and introduced in late 1968. It was for this model that the body designation was initially coined.

Break

A Break is an estate car in French bodywork nomenclature.

Squareback *(US)*

A self-explanatory term that is rapidly spreading in usage in the United States, squareback is fundamentally a straightforward synonym for station wagon. However, it is applied particularly to the rear-engined Volkswagen estate cars of the Type 3 and 411/412 varieties, although in some circles it is gaining ground over the older terminology for indigenous station wagons.

Part 2
Coachbuilders and their work

Automobile body design

COACHBUILDERS AND THEIR WORK
A coachbuilding company existed essentially to design and hand-build a body on a commission basis to the order of any customer, be he a private individual, a motor manufacturing or retail concern, civil authority, head of state, a member of the nobility or gentry, et al, the principal and most obvious proviso being his ability to settle the account on completion of an order (as indeed is so in any form of commerce).

The length of time taken to complete a commission depended on a multiplicity of factors, not the least being the manufacture and fitting of special features to the customer's stipulation. Persons connected with the coachbuilding business can recount manifold tales of weird and wonderful requests, ranging from the provision of a full set of dashboard instruments in the rear compartment (the ultimate in back-seat driving!), to colour-keying exterior paintwork to match an article of clothing (the latter perhaps fading before the bodywork was finished, necessitating an entire re-paint), and the employment of heraldic artists who were not only skilled in the painting of heraldic devices on door and side panels, but in addition were resourceful enough to design from scratch individual devices for those clients not entitled to recognised coats-of-arms.

Broadly speaking, English coachwork was celebrated for solidity, well-balanced lines and workmanship of the highest quality; English coachbuilders have always been acknowledged as pastmasters in the art of formal bodywork design and execution. French *Carrossiers* (coachbuilders: also *Carrosserie,* translating both as 'bodywork' and 'coachbuilding company') tended towards exuberant flamboyance and ornamentation at one extreme, to undistinguished dullness at the other, whilst the Germans built stolid, often rather brutal-looking bodies. The British and French coachbuilding industries reigned supreme in the field of ingenuity and elegance of design between the wars, whereas after 1945 the leadership was assumed by Italian *Carrozzeria,* a position currently maintained although rather tenuously of late.

American coachbuilders, otherwise *Custom Body Builders,* were relatively insulated from the influence of European design characteristics; nonetheless they produced plentiful examples of superb appearance and execution, especially on powerful chassis (Packard, Pierce-Arrow, Duesenberg, etc) that equalled the best that Britain and Europe could offer.

In order to provoke a conception of the many thousands of distinctive designs created over the last eighty-odd years I have selected examples emanating from fifty-five British and foreign coachbuilders, together with a very brief biographical outline on each company.

Some of these bodies are more elegant than others, depending on one's 'aesthetic eye', and several are rather ugly, but all share one common denominator: individuality. A commodity sadly lacking in today's mass-produced 'tinware'. However, there is no gainsaying that this individuality was fulfilled at a price; these bodies were not cheap in their heyday, and any single one would be astronomically expensive to build at today's prices.

Arnold   (England)

Based in Manchester, William Arnold commenced coachbuilding on automobile chassis in 1910, ceasing therefrom in 1948. Latterly the company has been connected with the motor retail trade.

Illustration: Saloon, 1934

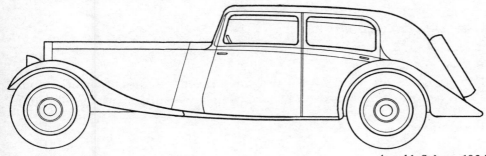

Arnold, Saloon 1934

Barker   (England)

Established in 1710, Barker and Co (Coachbuilders) Ltd of London was a highly-esteemed company that counted many members of British and foreign royalty amongst its patrons long before the motoring age dawned. The first Barker car body was built in 1905 (for the Hon. C.S. Rolls, of Rolls-Royce), the first of many - all of supreme workmanship - until the company went into liquidation in 1938, following which it was purchased by Messrs Hoopers. Barker continued to build bodies for Daimler, under Daimler ownership, until 1954.

Illustrations: Sedanca de Ville, 1933
Sedanca de Ville, 1936

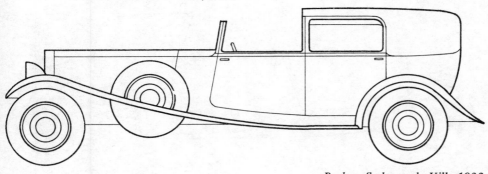

Barker, Sedanca de Ville 1933   73

Automobile body design

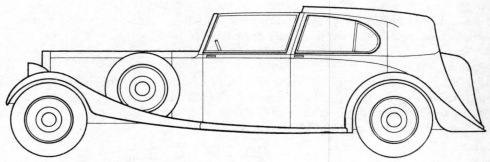

Barker, Sedanca de Ville 1936

Binder   (France)

Carrosserie Henri Binder of Paris commenced motor coachwork around 1904, ceasing operations in 1939. The company is still extant, but in another field.

Illustrations: Coupe de Ville, 1933
Sedanca Coupe, 1935

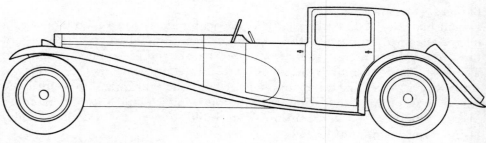

Binder, Coupe de Ville 1933

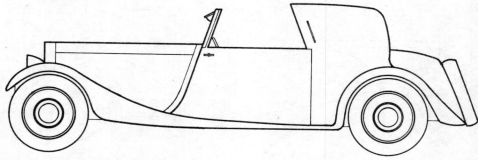

Binder, Sedanca Coupe 1935

Brewster   (United States)

Brewster and Co of Connecticut and latterly New York, was established in 1810. The first Brewster car body was built in 1905; the agency for Rolls-Royce cars was added to agencies for other marques under the Brewster wing in 1914. The company was purchased by Rolls-Royce of America Inc. - the US subsidiary of the parent English company - in 1926, thereafter building bodies exclusively for that firm until its demise in 1931. Brewster finally closed its doors for good in 1937.

Illustration: Roadster, 1929

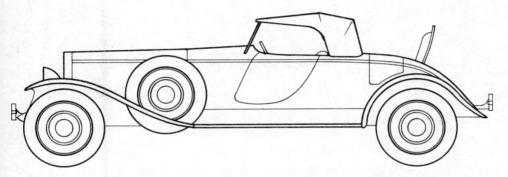

Brewster, Roadster 1929

Carbodies   (England)

Carbodies of Coventry was founded in 1926; it was bought by the BSA (Birmingham Small Arms) Group in 1954.

Illustration: Sports Saloon, 1933

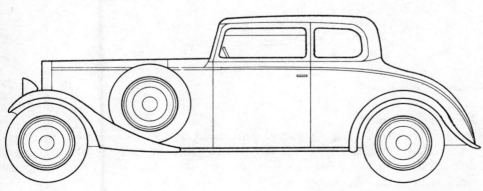

Carbodies, Sports Saloon 1933   75

Automobile body design

Carlton   (England)
Established in 1926, the Carlton Carriage Co Ltd of Willesden, London, produced motor car bodies until 1939. The company ceased operations altogether in 1965.
Illustration: Sports Saloon, 1930

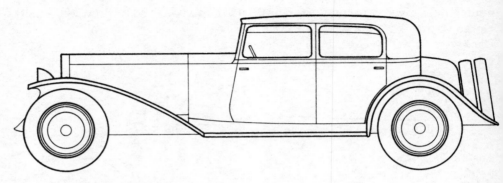

Carlton, Sports Saloon 1930

Castagna   (Italy)
This Milanese firm produced many superbly-shaped bodies, principally upon Alfa Romeo and Isotta Fraschini chassis. Production was resumed only for a short period after the Second World War.
Illustration: Cabriolet, 1929

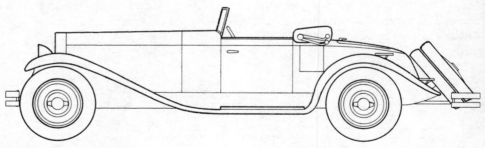

Castagna, Cabriolet 1929

Chapron   (France)
Henri Chapron of Paris created elegant, bold designs - especially on Delage and Delahaye chassis - from the late 1920s until the early 1950s, thereafter concentrating on adaptations of standard production cars. The company remains very much in existence.

76   *Illustration:*   Cabriolet, 1948

Chapron, Cabriolet 1948

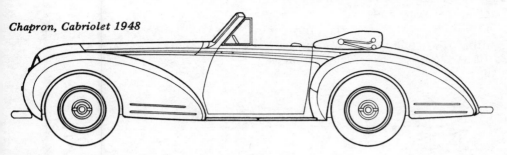

Charlesworth   (England)

Charlesworth Bodies Ltd of Coventry were noted for their smart Alvis Saloons and Drop-Head Coupes of the 1930s. Operations were not restarted after World War II.
Illustration: Drop-Head Coupe, 1938

Charlesworth, Drop-Head Coupe 1938

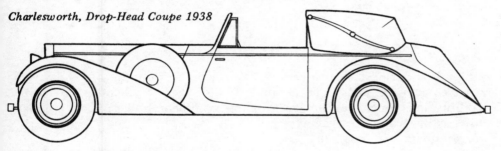

Cockshoot   (England)

Founded in 1844, Joseph Cockshoot and Co Ltd, Manchester, first constructed a car body in 1903. After building decreasing numbers of bodies during the late 1920s and the 1930s the company withdrew from coach-building in 1945, becoming Rolls-Royce and Bentley retailers.
Illustration: Landaulette, 1913.

Cockshoot, Landaulette 1913

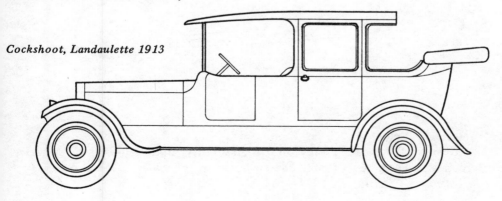

Automobile body design

Corsica   (England)
Corsica of Cricklewood concentrated chiefly on the creation of dashing
drop-head coupe styles during the 1930s.
Illustration: Drop-Head Coupe, 1931

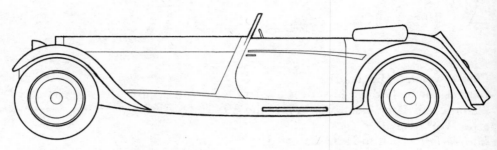

Corsica, Drop-Head Coupe 1931

Derham   (United States)
Established during the 19th century, the Derham Body Co. of Pennsylvania
was reorganised after the Second World War to handle coachwork
modifications only, no longer building complete bodies. The company
thrives still, as a motor agency.
Illustration: Tourer, 1935

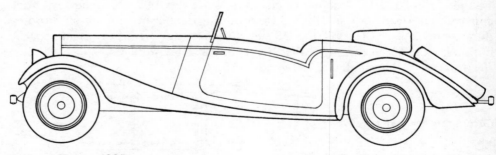

Derham, Tourer 1935

D'Ieteren   (Belgium)
The firm of D'Ieteren Freres built high-quality, luxury bodies on Minerva,
Mercedes-Benz and other large chassis between the wars.

Illustration: Cabriolet, 1928

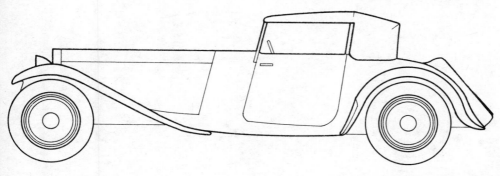

D'Ieteren, Cabriolet 1928

Erdmann & Rossi   (Germany)

Erdmann and Rossi specialised principally in Cabriolet bodywork of heavy yet well-proportioned lines.
Illustration: Cabriolet, 1927

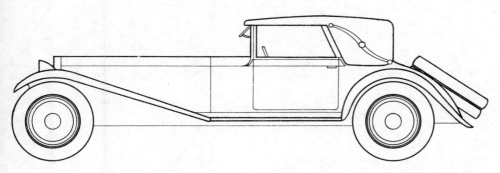

Erdmann & Rossi, Cabriolet 1927

Farina   (Italy)

Founded in Turin in 1926 by Battista ('Pinin') Farina, the house of Farina - renamed *Pininfarina* in 1958 - is the foremost Italian car design and limited-production company. Commencing with Lancias, Farina has clothed a very wide variety of chassis in the past 50 years; the criterion for post-World War II styling was set by the famous Cisitalia Coupe, and the latest design for an English manufacturer graces the Rolls-Royce Camargue, presently the world's most expensive car.
Illustration: Coupe, 1946

79

Automobile body design

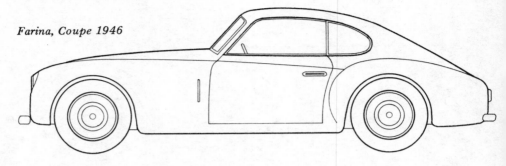

Farina, Coupe 1946

Fernandez et Darrin   (France)

A partnership between financier Fernandez and American designer Howard Darrin, this company was initiated in 1932 as successor to the Hibbard et Darrin concern. After producing many notable bodies of considerable flamboyance and excellent execution, the works closed down in 1939.
Illustration: Open Drive Limousine, 1938

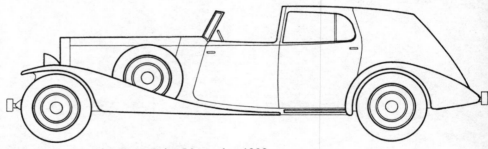

Fernandez et Darrin, Open Drive Limousine 1938

Figoni et Falaschi   (France)

This concern specialised in spectacular designs on a variety of chassis types and sizes. It disappeared after World War II.
Illustration: Coupe, 1937

Figoni et Falaschi, Coupe 1937

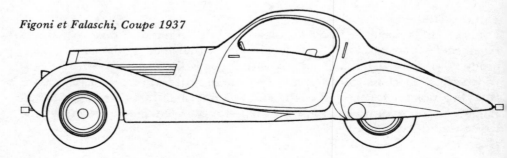

80

Flewitt   (England)

Flewitt Ltd of Birmingham was established in 1905 and produced coachbuilt bodies consistently until 1957, though only in very small quantities after 1945. Beyond 1957 the company concentrated on motor repairs.

Illustration: Single Landaulette, 1923.

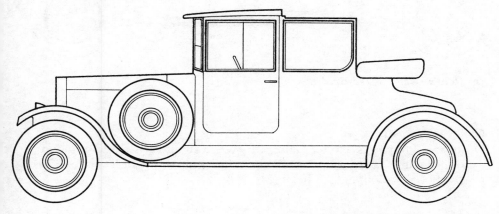

Flewitt, Single Landaulette 1923

Freestone and Webb   (England)

Freestone and Webb Ltd was established in Willesden, London, as a coachbuilding concern in 1923. The company rapidly became renowned for bodywork of high quality and good design, a reputation maintained until final closure. The firm's two specialities were razor-edged features and top-hat saloons. Purchased by H.R. Owen Ltd, Rolls-Royce/Bentley retailers in 1955, Freestone and Webb ceased operations altogether in 1957.

Illustrations: Sedanca de Ville, 1930.
                    Fixed-Head Coupe, 1931

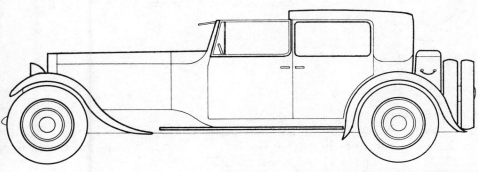

Freestone & Webb, Sedanca de Ville 1930   81

Automobile body design

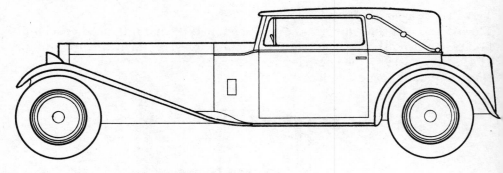

Freestone & Webb, Fixed-Head Coupe 1931

Galle   (France)
Otherwise known as Baxter-Galle, this was a small Paris-based company that produced solid, fairly sober coachwork throughout the 1920s and 1930s.
Illustration: Coupe de Ville, 1930

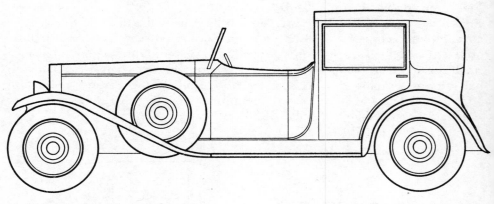

Galle, Coupe de Ville 1930

Gill   (England)
The coachbuilders T.H. Gill and Son Ltd of Paddington, London, specialised in the production of all-weather bodies. The first Gill body was constructed in 1914; the company closed down in 1935.
Illustration: All-Weather Tourer, 1930

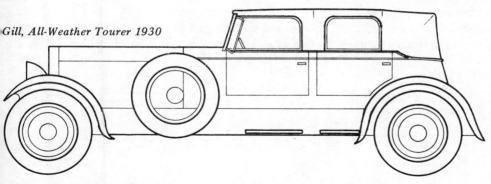

Gill, All-Weather Tourer 1930

Gurney Nutting   (England)

The famed coachbuilding company of J. Gurney Nutting and Co Ltd was founded in London in 1919. The excellence in design and construction of Gurney Nutting coachwork attracted many members of British royalty, amongst a host of notables; the bodies for Sir Malcolm Campbell's 'Bluebird' land speed record cars were built by this firm. The company was acquired by Rolls-Royce/Bentley distributors, Jack Barclay Ltd, in 1945, thereupon terminating coachbuilding activities.

Illustrations: Saloon Coupe, 1930
Drop-Head Sedanca Coupe, 1934

Gurney Nutting, Saloon Coupe 1930

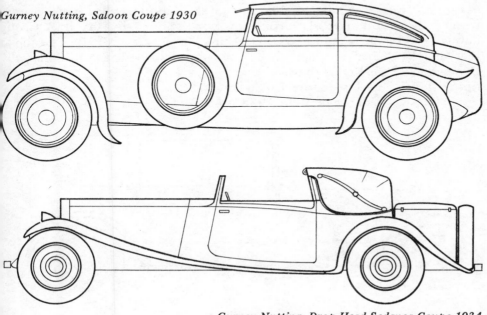

Gurney Nutting, Drop-Head Sedanca Coupe 1934   **83**

Automobile body design

Harrison (England)
Established in 1883, R. Harrison and Son Ltd created some stolid but good-looking formal bodies in the late 1920s. The company became defunct in 1931.
Illustration: Limousine, 1929

Harrison, Limousine 1929

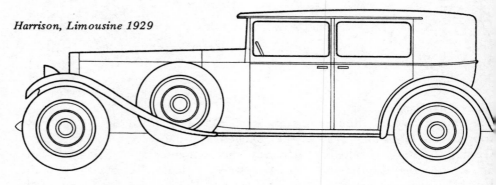

Hooper (England)
Arguably the most important company in British motor car coachbuilding history, Hooper and Co (Coachbuilders) Ltd of London was founded in 1805 and held a warrant as coachbuilders to the British Royal Family for an unrivalled 130 years, until closure in 1959. Hooper's stately, graceful and beautifully worked bodies resulted moreover in an unparalled patronage by royalty the world over. The company was acquired by the BSA Group during World War II and assigned to Daimler (also part of the BSA Group at that time), thereafter producing many top-class designs on principally Daimler and Rolls-Royce chassis.
Illustrations: Enclosed Drive Landaulette, 1926
Sedanca de Ville, 1938

Hooper, Enclosed Drive Landaulette 1926

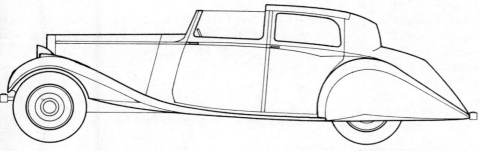

Hooper, Sedanca de Ville 1938

Jarvis   (England)

Jarvis of Wimbledon was a small coachbuilding concern, extant in the 1920s and early 1930s.

Illustration: Boat-Tailed Tourer, 1927

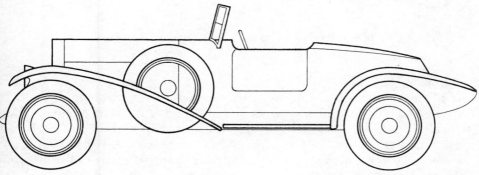

Jarvis, Boat-Tailed Tourer 1927

Kellner   (France)

Based in Paris, Kellner et Cie. created many magnificent bodies of formal and other styles, principally on Hispano-Suiza chassis, between the wars.

Illustration: Coupe Limousine, 1933

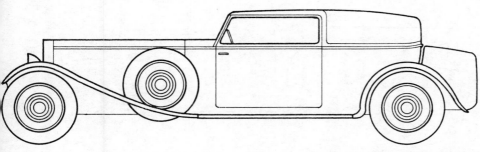

Kellner, Coupe Limousine 1933   85

Automobile body design

Lancefield   (England)
Lancefield Coachworks Ltd of London first produced a motor body in 1921;
the company continued coachbuilding activities until 1948, thereafter
switching allegiance to aircraft component manufacture.
Illustration: Sports Limousine, 1934

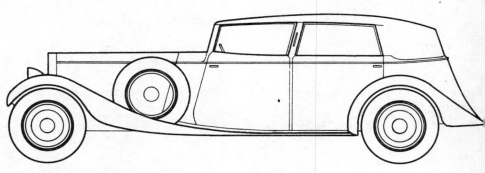

Lancefield, Sports Limousine 1934

LeBaron   (United States)
One of the most famous and probably the best of American coachbuilders,
LeBaron of Connecticut was founded in 1920. The company was
particularly adept at designing formal and semi-formal bodies. Coachwork
operations were halted in 1941, upon American entry into World War II, and
the company was purchased by the Chrysler Corporation in 1948; the name
LeBaron has since appeared many times on top-line Chrysler products,
though the company itself ceased to exist as coachbuilders after takeover.
Illustration: Town Cabriolet, 1930

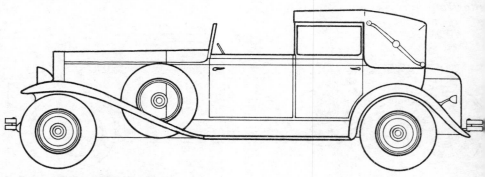

LeBaron, Town Cabriolet 1930

Letourneur et Marchand   (France)
A Paris-based company that began motor coachbuilding before World War I,
Letourneur et Marchand closed down at the outbreak of war in 1939 and did
not re-open.
Illustration: Faux Cabriolet, 1931

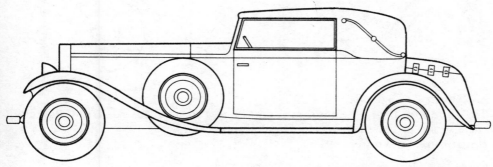

Letourneur et Marchand, Faux Cabriolet 1931

Mann Egerton   (England)
Mann, Egerton and Co Ltd was established in Norwich in 1898 and first
constructed a car body in 1901. The firm was reorganised after World War II
as an Austin (now British Leyland) distributorship.
Illustration: Saloon + division, 1939

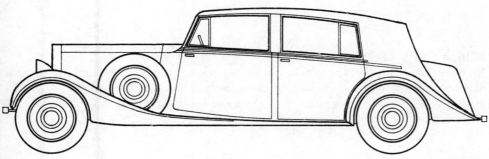

Mann Egerton, Saloon with Division 1939

Mayfair   (England)
Established in London in 1920 as the Progressive Carriage Co, with the name
changed to the Mayfair Carriage Co Ltd in 1929, Mayfair produced motor
bodies up till 1939 and recommenced after World War II as builders of
commercial vehicle coachwork. In 1959 the company was reconstituted as a
motor service and repair centre.
Illustration: Drop-Head Coupe, 1936

87

Automobile body design

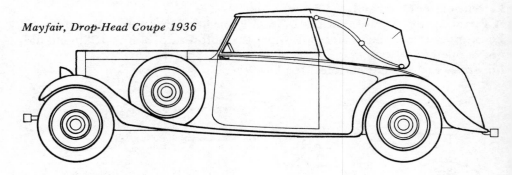

Mayfair, Drop-Head Coupe 1936

Maythorn   (England)
The London firm of Maythorn and Son Ltd was founded in 1842, but succumbed in 1931 during the Great Depression.
Illustration: Tourer, 1925

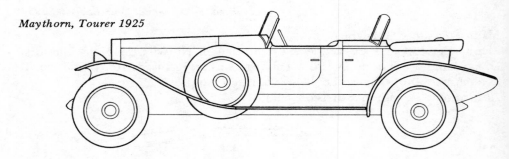

Maythorn, Tourer 1925

Million Guiet   (France)
Million Guiet of Paris created some striking bodies on Hispano-Suiza, Mercedes-Benz and other large chassis during the 1920s and early 1930s. After World War II, motor car coachbuilding was halted in favour of commercial vehicle coachwork.
Illustration: Cabriolet, 1930

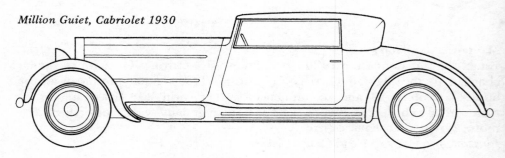

Million Guiet, Cabriolet 1930

Arthur Mulliner   (England)
Inaugurated in the 18th century, Arthur Mulliner Ltd of Northampton began
to design automobile bodies in the 1890s and continued to produce
coachwork until the outbreak of war in 1939. The firm was purchased by
the motor distributors Henly's Ltd closing in 1976 after many years in the
retail motor business.
Illustration: Saloon, 1929

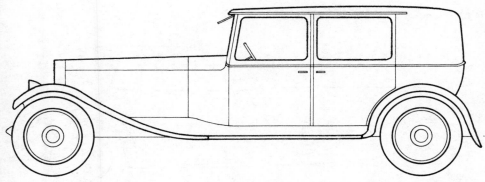

Arthur Mulliner, Saloon 1929

H.J. Mulliner   (England)
H.J. Mulliner and Co Ltd of Chiswick, London, was formed in 1900 through
the acquisition by Mr. H.J. Mulliner from his relatives of the London branch
of Arthur Mulliner Ltd. The company rapidly became associated with top-
class workmanship and high standards of design, assuming a leading position
in the British coachbuilding industry; H.J. Mulliner's formal and semi-formal
Rolls-Royce bodies of the 1920s and 1930s were all but unmatched in grace
and magnificence. The company was sold to the coachbuilders Croall of
Edinburgh in 1914, and the production level between the wars was very high
compared to other coachworks. After building many memorable bodies on
Rolls-Royce chassis after 1945, H.J. Mulliner was acquired by Rolls-Royce
Ltd in 1959 and merged with the Park Ward coachworks in 1961, the
resultant company being known as H.J. Mulliner, Park Ward Ltd and based
in Willesden, London. This company currently produces the handbuilt
Rolls-Royce Corniche, Phantom VI and Rolls-Royce Camargue.
Illustrations: Coupe Sports Tourer, 1925
Sedanca de Ville, 1934.   89

Automobile body design

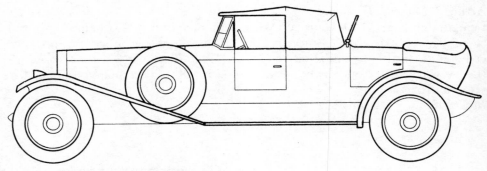

H.J. Mulliner, Coupe Sports Tourer 1925

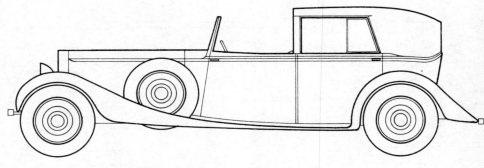

H.J. Mulliner, Sedanca de Ville 1934

Murphy   (United States)
The Walter M. Murphy Co was established in 1921 at Pasadena, California; the firm was noted for a variety of drop-head body styles. Trading ceased in 1933.
Illustration: Convertible Coupe, 1931

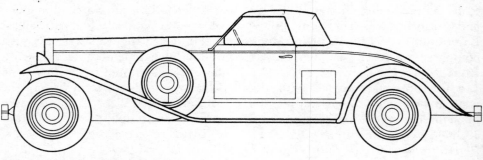

Murphy, Convertible Coupe 1931

Offord   (England)
Founded in Kensington, London in 1791, Offord and Sons Ltd first constructed an automobile body in 1896. Like so many other coachbuilders Offord's coachbuilding activities ceased in 1939; the company is currently a retail outlet for Rolls-Royce and Bentley motor cars.
Illustration: Coupe de Ville, 1933

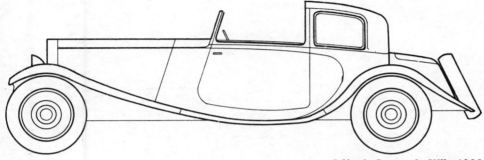

Offord, Coupe de Ville 1933

Papler   (Germany)
A German company known for its touring and cabriolet bodywork on large supercharged Mercedes-Benz chassis of the mid-1920s to early-1930s period.
Illustration: Tourer, 1928

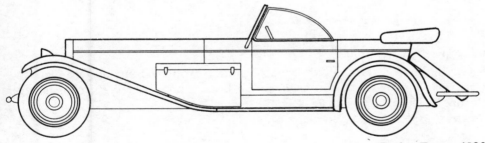

Papler, Tourer 1928

Park Ward   (England)
Formed in 1919, Park, Ward and Co Ltd of Willesden, London, established from the outset a close relationship with Rolls-Royce Ltd, on whose chassis were fitted the overriding majority of Park Ward coachwork. The firm was bought by Rolls-Royce in 1939, for whom thenceforward Park Ward designed bodies exclusively. Park Ward was amalgamated with H.J. Mulliner in 1961 to form H.J. Mulliner, Park Ward Ltd, which continues to handbuild Rolls-Royce bodies.
Illustrations: Boat-Tailed Tourer, 1929
                    Brougham de Ville, 1934

Automobile body design

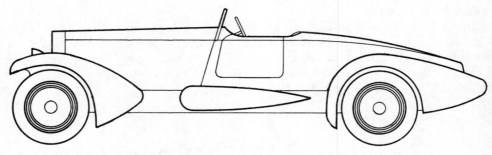

Park Ward, Boat-Tailed Tourer 1929

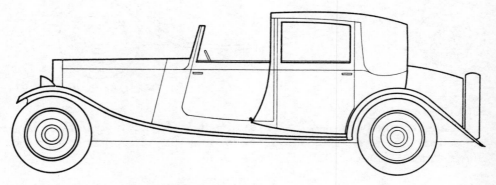

Park Ward, Brougham de Ville 1934

Ranalah   (England)

Based in Merton, Surrey, the coachbuilding firm of Ranalah designed and constructed primarily drop-head coupe bodies on a variety of chassis until closure in 1939.

Illustration: Drop-Head Coupe, 1935

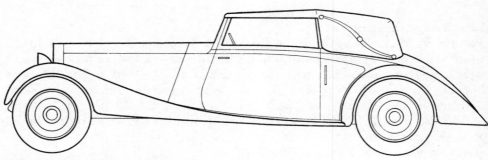

92   *Ranalah, Drop-Head Coupe 1935*

Rippon   (England)
One of the very oldest coachbuilding establishments - Rippon carriages were
fabricated for the aristocracy as long ago as the reign of Mary Tudor - the
Huddersfield firm of Rippon Bros. Ltd designed bodywork chiefly for Rolls-
Royce chassis; the initial Rippon automobile body appeared in 1905. Few
bodies were consrructed after World War II, and the company closed its
coachworks in 1958, concentrating thereafter on the retail of Rolls-Royce
and Bentley cars.
Illustration: Enclosed Drive Limousine, 1911

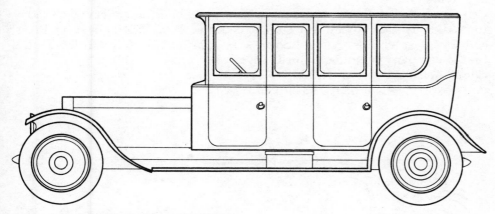

Rippon, Enclosed Drive Limousine 1911

Salmons   (England)
The first car body to appear from the Newport Pagnell works of Salmons
and Sons, established in 1820, was in 1907. During the 1920s and early
1930s Salmons were noted for their unusual saloon cabriolet coachwork and
in the later 1930s for drop-head bodies and 'Tickford' Saloons. Renamed
Tickford in 1940, the company produced coachwork on Lagonda chassis in
the late 1940s and 1950s, and was acquired by the David Brown
organisation, of which Lagonda was part, in 1957. Aston Martin cars are
manufactured in the former Salmons/Tickford plant.
Illustration: Saloon Cabriolet, 1930.

Automobile body design

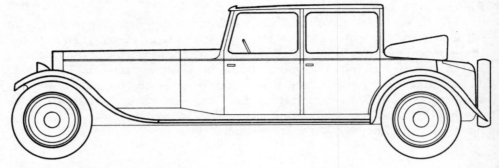

Salmons, Saloon Cabriolet 1930

Saoutchik   (France)

Carrosserie J. Saoutchik, founded in Paris in 1905, is remembered nowadays for strikingly flamboyant yet elegant coachwork on large, powerful British and European chassis. A few bodies were constructed after World War II up till the company's liquidation in 1954.

Illustrations: Phaeton, 1926
                   Cabriolet, 1934

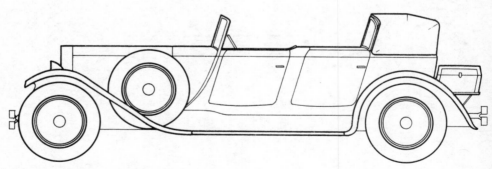

Saoutchik, Phaeton 1926

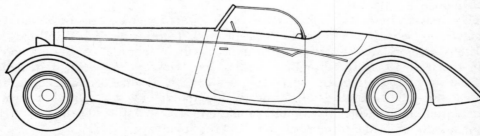

94   *Saoutchik, Cabriolet 1934*

Thrupp and Maberly   (England)
Founded in 1760, Thrupp and Maberly Ltd of London commenced automobile coachbuilding in the 1890s, and in the years between the Wars specialised in bodies for large chassis. The company was bought by the Rootes Group in 1925, and in 1946 it was reorganised, thereafter mass-producing body shells for the Group and subsequently for Chrysler.
Illustrations: Drop-Head Coupe, 1930
                    Saloon, 1935

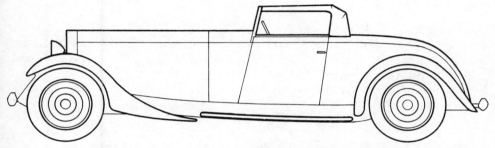

Thrupp & Maberly, Drop-Head Coupe 1930

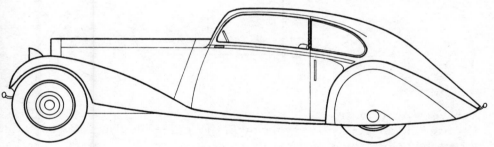

Thrupp & Maberly, Saloon 1935

Vanden Plas   (England)
Established in 1912 as an offshoot of the Belgian coachbuilders of the same name, Vanden Plas (originally Van den Plas - through common usage the first two words were conjoined) constructed few bodies before World War I; during the war and for some years afterwards the company manufactured aircraft fuselages, until being reconstituted as a coachworks in 1923. Vanden Plas (England) 1923 Ltd, as it was then titled, was famed for drop-head and touring bodies, notably those touring bodies fitted to Vintage Bentley chassis. After purchase by the Austin Motor Co in 1946 the firm commenced to construct limousines, and also to produce semi-handbuilt models for Austin (subsequently BMC and BLMC) by outfitting mass-produced models with coachbuilt appurtenances, roles that Vanden Plas continues to fulfil today.
Illustration: Cabriolet, 1937

Automobile body design

Vanden Plas, Cabriolet 1937

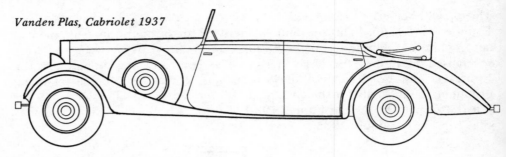

Van den Plas   (Belgium)
Carrosserie Van den Plas S.A. was an old-established (1868) coachbuilding concern that built chiefly open body styles into the 1930s. The company folded before the Second World War.
Illustration: Torpedo, 1926

Van den Plas, Torpedo 1926

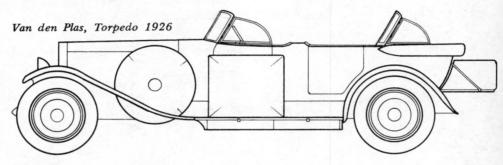

Van Vooren   (France)
Carrosserie Van Vooren (or Vanvooren) of Courbevoie, Paris created a wide variety of body designs in the years between the two World Wars. Some Van Vooren bodies approached Saoutchik in flamboyance and elan, but many were staid though well-executed closed bodies on medium-sized chassis. The firm closed down in 1939.
Illustration: Saloon, 1930

Van Vooren, Saloon 1930

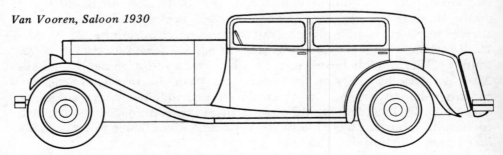

Vesters and Neirinck   (Belgium)
A small Brussels-based coachbuilding company, Vesters and Neirinck built some remarkably fine coupe and touring bodies during the 1930s.
Illustration: Torpedo, 1938

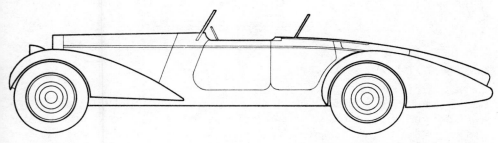

Vesters & Neirinck, Torpedo 1938

Vincents   (England)
Now motor retail distributors, Vincents of Reading were founded as coachbuilders in 1805 and built both motor car and commercial vehicle bodies until the late 1950s.
Illustration: Enclosed Drive Limousine, 1930

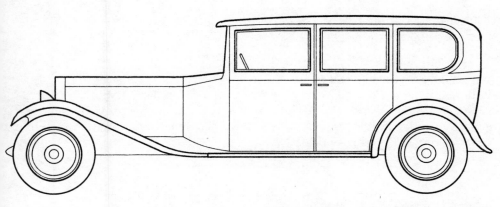

Vincents, Enclosed Drive Limousine 1930

Walter, Martin   (England)
Martin Walter Ltd of Folkestone, Kent constructed coachbuilt bodies until 1939, thereafter concentrating on outfitting vans and motor caravans in addition to business as a motor retail agency.
Illustration: Fixed-Head Coupe, 1930   **97**

Automobile body design

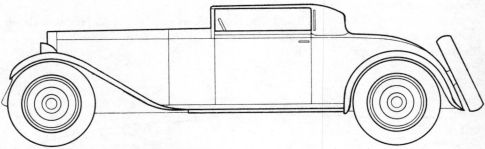

Martin Walter, Fixed-Head Coupe 1930

Weymann   (France)
Bodies constructed under Weymann patents during the 1920s and 1930s were not only fabricated at the parent Weymann coachworks in Paris, but also by an English branch at Addlestone, Surrey, and by numerous licensees in Britain and Europe.
Illustration: Fixed-Head Coupe, 1930

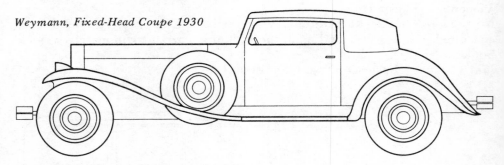

Weymann, Fixed-Head Coupe 1930

Willoughby   (United States)
Willoughby and Co of Utica, New York, were established shortly after the First World War and closed in the late 1930s. Willoughby bodies were generally sober in concept yet often contained superbly appointed interiors.
Illustration: Touring Cabriolet, 1937

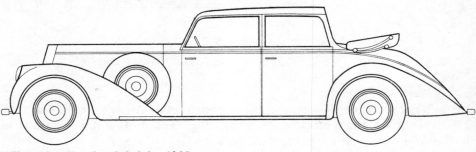

Willoughby, Touring Cabriolet 1937

Windovers   (England)

Founded in London in 1796, Windovers Ltd enjoyed an unprecedented clientele amongst Indian potentates for automobile bodies before and after the First World War. Based mainly on Rolls-Royce chassis before World War II, Windovers built few car bodies after 1945, their efforts being redirected towards commercial vehicle coachwork in the post-war years. The company was purchased by Henly's Ltd in 1956.

Illustration: Sedanca de Ville, 1933.

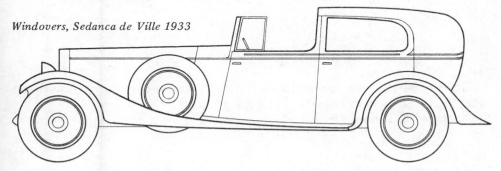

Windovers, Sedanca de Ville 1933

James Young   (England)

Another leading English coachbuilder, James Young and Co Ltd of Bromley, Kent, established in 1863, commenced motor coachwork in 1908. Renowned for superbly designed and executed Rolls-Royce bodies before and after World War II, James Young also created some sporting coupes and tourers on a number of chassis in the 1930s. After the Second World War, having been acquired by Rolls-Royce/Bentley distributors Jack Barclay Ltd in 1937, the company applied its coachcraft exclusively to Rolls-Royce and Bentley chassis. The company was reconstituted in 1967 and now undertakes coachwork restoration and repairs.

Illustrations: Sports Saloon, 1934
Saloon Coupe, 1939.

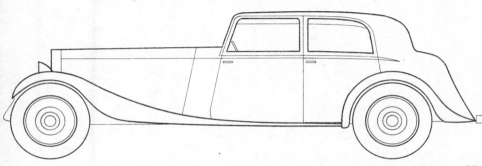

James Young, Sports Saloon 1934   99

Automobile body design

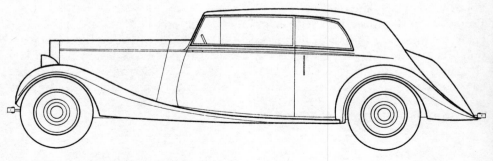

James Young, Saloon Coupe 1939

Zietz   (Switzerland)
A Geneva-based company remembered for coachbuilt touring bodies on supercharged Mercedes-Benz K, S and SS chassis.
Illustration: Tourer, 1927

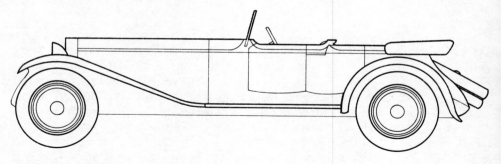

Zietz, Tourer 1927

100

Part 3
The evolution of styling

Automobile body design

THE EVOLUTION OF STYLING

Of the manifold types of body that have been devised in the ninety-year history of the automobile, whether transposed and adapted from horse-drawn conveyances or designed and developed from the outset as indigenous motor bodies, of the seemingly endless diversity of shapes and sizes, of the exuberance or dignity, the plainness or turgidity that these body types inspired, the majority vanished in the onslaught of mass-produced uniformity that left in its wake just a handful of basic body types which we recognise in today's cars: the saloon, the estate car, the coupe, the open sports car and the occasional limousine.

As social divisions became increasingly blurred after the Second World War and it was no longer mandatory or even desirable for the nobility and gentry to 'show' themselves to the now disinterested public at large, so body types of landaulette and similar form disappeared from the roads (excepting those still built individually for sovereigns and heads of state). The economics of employing and housing a full-time chauffeur are now prohibitive for all but exceedingly wealthy individuals or large companies, a factor that in conjunction with the wide and nowadays less tolerated distinction between a chauffeur and his employer (a continuation of the former 'master-servant' relationship) inherent in a formal-bodied car - physically separated by a glass division ('to keep the smell of the driver at bay', as an elderly acquaintance put it), the owner is ensconced in luxury in the rear compartment whilst the paid driver is lodged in comparative discomfort behind the steering wheel - has ensured the gradual and continuing decline in construction of large, opulent limousines. Due in some measure to its opening front roof which exacerbated the sociological employer-employee discrepancy, the sedanca de ville style is now extinct.

Whilst the constant rise in standards of living in the past twenty-five years has created ever-widening markets for reasonably priced and therefore mass-produced cars, the increasing cost of craftsmanship consequent upon this rise has - amongst other factors - resulted in a decreased demand for coachbuilt cars, thus forcing erstwhile coachbuilding companies into liquidation or into fundamental diversification of their activities.

In order to portray the development of body design over several decades, by way of text coupled with illustrations, I have chosen ten body types representative of those employed to a greater or lesser extent by motor manufacturers and coachbuilders from the termination of the Second World War to the present day; these bodies will therefore be at least fairly familiar to modern-car buffs. Two such body types (the aforementioned sedanca de ville, and the four-door cabriolet) are no longer fabricated but are included here because their development was parallel with and complementary over a similar period to the other eight styles; additionally, although the modern examples given here for four of the ten body types are no longer called by the titles under which they are placed, and indeed may not be of strictly the correct configuration as originally propounded for these styles, they conform at least in spirit with their predecessors. These instances will be identified as they arise.

1 Saloon

In terms of production quantity the saloon is by far and away the most popular body style ever devised, having remained so from 1930 or thereabouts on succeeding the open tourer as the most practicable format from both the manufacturing and consumer points of view. The multi-national motor manufacturers Ford, General Motors and Chrysler, and large national companies such as British Leyland, Fiat and Renault depend on their saloon products as the mainstay of their sales - the 'bread and butter' of the industry - using a percentage of the income derived therefrom to subsidise coupe and estate car variants based upon saloon body panels and running gear.

The total output of the World's coachbuilding industry from the late 1920s to the outbreak of hostilities in 1939 was but a miniscule fraction of the immense outpourings of mass-produced cars throughout the same period; this fact, coupled with the fact that saloons figured to a much lesser degree in coachbuilders' design catalogues than in those of mass-manufacturing companies, meant that in terms of sheer numbers handbuilt saloon cars hardly made a startling impact on the roads of industrialized nations. Their influence in terms of design was another matter, however.

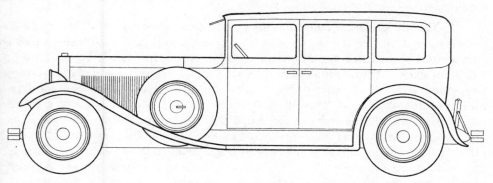

Figure 1 Adaptation from 1929 Mercedes-Benz Nurburg

Figure 1 shows the typical square-rigged shape of the late 1920s; most medium-to-large saloons prior to World War II were six-light, as this is. The specification of this example (adapted from a 1929 Nurburg-model Mercedes-Benz) includes spring bumpers which, unlike more modern bumpers, possess sufficient elasticity to absorb quite hefty shocks with

103

impunity; they are positioned some distance from the bodywork on mountings attached directly to the chassis frame. Bumpers in the true sense of the word. The then-customary lack of luggage accommodation within the confines of the body is evidenced by the provision of a folding grid at the rear whilst the spare wheel is side-mounted, an alternative and very common arrangement to rear-mounting. The typical vertical windscreen that could be opened to ventilate the car was a throwback to much earlier and less sophisticated days; windscreen wipers had made their debut a few years before 1929 but sloping windscreens were not to become general until well into the 1930s. Interior heaters and demisters were unknown in the late 1920s and for long afterwards, so that opening windscreens remained common until well after World War II. Many cars were fitted with glass vizors under the leading edge of the roof, as on this example, to assist in maintaining a reasonably clean windscreen surface by deflecting raindrops.

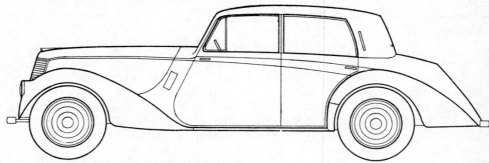

Figure 2 Armstrong Siddeley Whitley, 1948

The progress of Saloon design over the twenty years from 1929 is demonstrated in *Figure 2,* in which the full wings and less severe, more curvaceous body lines are immediately apparent. The late 1940s and early 1950s marked a transitional period in which the pre-war format of separate wings and somewhat upright body lines began to evolve into the modern idiom of the four-light 'three-box' configuration (bonnet, passenger cabin and boot) where the wings are integrated into the body proper. This example, an Armstrong Siddeley Whitley of 1949 vintage, shows that the effect of the inclusion of a reasonably capacious enclosed boot is to make the body more close-coupled: the rear-seat passengers are no longer situated behind the rear axle line and the rear legroom is reduced accordingly. A by-product of this close-coupling is an improved ride for the rear passengers: because the rear seat is within the wheelbase it is less affected by the amplitude of rear suspension motion. The body sides have become broader, so that the rear wings are now part of the body sides, and the running-board (the footplate connecting front and rear wings) is much narrower; the still-prominent front wings are attached to the body sides as opposed to the chassis and feature headlamps fared into their forward surfaces. The bumpers are not so shock-resistant as formerly and the bonnet is hinged at its rear edge to open in alligator fashion, rather than hinged along the bonnet centre-line as on pre-war cars. Finally this example, as many other English Saloons at the time, is semi razor-edged and swivelling front quarter lights have appeared as standard fitments.

Figure 3   Rover 75, 1955

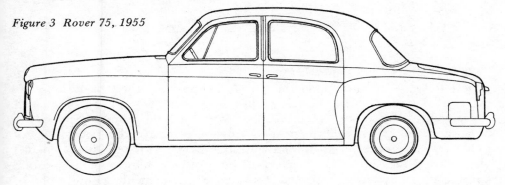

The wings of the next specimen (*Figure 3*) are all but wholly integrated into the body sides, the sole remaining vestiges of the pre-war style being the sculptured panels and the pronounced shape forward of the front wheel arch, where the area between the wing line and radiator grille is reminiscent of the former total division between radiator and wing. The width of the body sides now comprises the width of the car, the boot is square-shaped and much larger and the bumpers, whilst being fairly substantial, are no longer shock-absorbent. The windscreen and rear window (in this instance the latter is composed of three sections) are made of curved safety glass - the technique of manufacturing curved glazing was perfected in the 1950s, notwithstanding which troublesome distortions due to curvature still occur all too frequently in present-day cars - and the running-board has disappeared for good. The car illustrated in *Figure 3* is a 1955-model Rover 75; affectionately called 'Auntie Rovers', these were sedate but well-constructed and finely-appointed cars, not endowed with sparkling acceleration though possessed of considerable staying power once a speed was reached. These Rovers were built over a period of fifteen years, in a succession of engine sizes and transmission variations.

A representative example of a modern Saloon is to be found in *Figure 4*, the 'New Generation' Mercedes-Benz 250 introduced in 1968 and in quantity production today in slightly modified form. Mercedes-Benz is one of the few marques still to retain an immediately recognisable radiator shell; it is very much wider and more squat than those on former models of this marque, in order to be compatible with the low, broad body style. All trace of wings in the former sense has now vanished; however, those side

Automobile body design

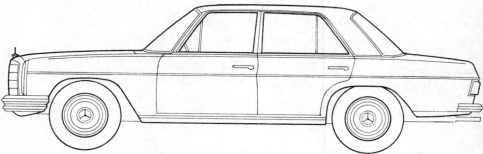

Figure 4 Mercedes-Benz 250, 1968

panels forward of and behind the doors incorporating the wheel arches are universally termed 'wing panels'. The total window area has increased considerably over saloon designs of the 1950s, the bonnet and boot deck are broad and almost flat, and the whole is now of 'three-box' configuration. All four doors are front-hinged to eliminate the danger of their being wrenched off by wind pressure or impact should they accidentally open at speed; a sensible feature which is a partial result of an ever-expanding philosophy of vehicular safety, applicative spin-offs from which range from the eminently sensible through the absurd to the downright dangerous.

2 Sports Saloon

The sports saloon underwent - as indeed have all the body types considered here - a similar styling transformation to the conventional saloon since the former's introduction in the late 1920s. Common prior to the Second World War in its original format, ie a four-door, four-light close-coupled saloon of sporting pretensions, the term sports saloon has been applied but infrequently since 1945, yet many saloons manufactured in the past three decades could very well be called sports saloons by virtue of sleek flowing lines allied with powerful engines and superior roadholding-handling characteristics. So far as Britain is concerned, the various Jaguar saloons built from 1950 to date are obvious candidates for the title sports saloon, and accordingly two Jaguars are illustrated here.

Figure 5 displays the archetypal early sports saloon; a long bonnet, sloping windscreen, relatively small passenger area and sports-car type individual wings attest to its sporting demeanour. Further points of divergence from a straightforward saloon of the period are the inclusion of an enclosed boot and small step-plates beneath the doors in lieu of a full-length running-board which are slotted into a louvred valance covering the chassis frame.

Only seven years mark the age differential between the model in *Figure 5,* (a 1930 Sports Saloon by Victor Broom) and that depicted in *Figure 6,* a Vanden Plas body from 1937, yet what an extraordinarily rapid

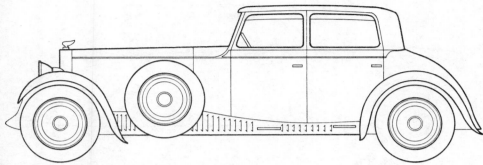

Figure 5 Sports Saloon, Victor Broom, 1930

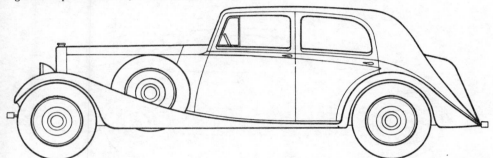

Figure 6 Sports Saloon, Vanden Plas, 1937

advance has taken place in those seven short years! The body is altogether more fluid, a more cohesive juxtaposition of wings, bonnet and passenger cabin; the swept front wings feature aprons behind the wheels to reduce tyre-splash, and front quarter lights are fitted, although these were not to become widespread until after World War II. In many ways this body is akin to the post-war Mk.VI Bentley Standard Saloon, so that sports saloon styling of the mid-1930s could be looked upon as precursive of conventional Saloon styling of the late 1940s.

The sensational Mk VII Jaguar, featured in *Figure 7,* first appeared before the public in 1950; it was a car of brilliant conception whose superbly voluptuous lines belied its substantial size and weight. The massive wing line altogether dominates the design, the frontal aspect harks back to pre-war practice in the use of a tall vertically-barred radiator grille flanked by swaged panels (in this instance encasing the headlamps and a pair of driving lamps) and the bulbous front wing contours, and the roof panel features a subtle turn-under that harmonises with the sharply radiused rear door light. The rear wheel spats greatly assist in streamlining the shape, and the sloping boot panel maintains the sweeping effect created by the wing line. In sum, a styling tour de force, reinforced by an impressively high performance, that was not transcended for several years.

107

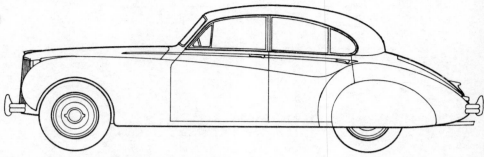

Figure 7 Jaguar Mk VII, 1952

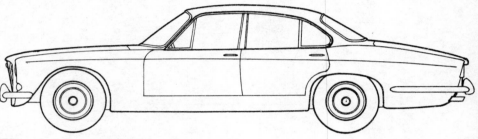

Figure 8 Jaguar XJ6, 1968

The modern successor to the Mk VII Jaguar is the justly-renowned Jaguar XJ6 Saloon, shown in *Figure 8,* which, like its forerunner, is a car of no mean bulk. Initially introduced at the latter end of 1968, the XJ6 is of basically 'three-box' configuration yet exhibits much more markedly curved panels and rounded edges than are generally apparent in present-day Saloons; indeed it amply demonstrates the individuality of design that has always been a Jaguar tradition. Almost all pretence at delineating a wing line in the former sense has gone, yet the shape is characterised by a definite horizontal contour, paralleled by the bonnet and bootlid surfaces, that runs from atop the headlamp rearwards, rises succinctly over the rear wheel arch and terminates in a reverse slope incorporating the rear lamp assembly at the back of the car. For all its length the XJ6 is rather more close-coupled than the Mk VII Jaguar though the window area, by dint of a large windscreen and rear window, is greatly increased over the latter. Furnished with more than adequate performance, tenacious roadholding and handling characteristics and a high degree of interior comfort in addition to its evocative appearance, the XJ6 can with every justification be termed a sports saloon.

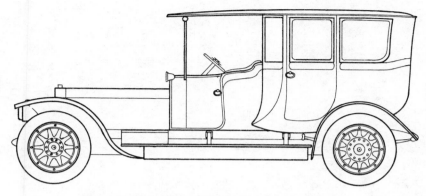

Figure 9 Rolls-Royce Silver Ghost Cockshoot Limousine, 1911

3 Limousine

The initial example of a limousine *(Figure 9)* stems from an earlier period than those bodies we have scrutinised thus far; the Cockshoot coachwork on a 1911 Rolls-Royce Silver Ghost chassis depicts all the quintessential components of an Edwardian limousine. Several major features are immediately apparent: first and foremost the open drive front compartment, complete with unshielded sides, though doors, roof and a tall windscreen are provided. The scuttle rises abruptly aft of the low bonnet, a characteristic shared with many other Edwardian bodies (compare the bonnet height with that depicted in *Figure 10*), the front compartment is backed by a D-front partition which unfortunately is not effectively portrayed in a side-view illustration, and the tulip-shaped back panel sets the tone of the rear compartment - the panel outline is repeated in the quarter light frame, the door panel and lower section of the D-front partition to render a distinctly carriage-like aspect to the rear half of the body. Due to the very considerable turn-under of the base of the back panel, the rear seat would needs be mounted at quite a height inside the compartment, necessitating in turn tall body sides. A top hat was still part of a gentleman's everyday attire in 1911, so that the body height requirement was doubly necessary to accommodate occupants thus adorned. Wooden artillery wheels were frequent fitments on early Edwardian cars, though by 1911 they were beginning to be supplanted by the ubiquitous wire-spoked wheels which remained standard fittings on most expensive chassis (except in the United States where artillery wheels were common till the early 1930s) up to 1939. Coachbuilders tended to mask the spokes with all-enveloping metal covers, especially on formal-bodied cars, to achieve cleaner profiles. Pressed-steel disc wheels in the form we know them today first appeared for general usage in the early 1920s on mass-produced cars; the vast majority of cars built since 1945 have been so equipped.

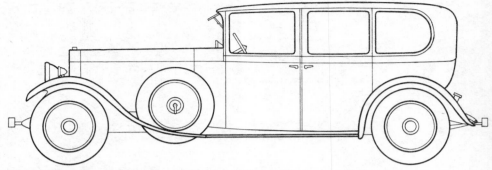

Figure 10 Rolls-Royce Phantom II Barker Pullman Limousine, 1929

Turning to *Figure 10,* we notice straight away that this limousine is not so tall as, and is much smoother in appearance than the 1911 car, and moreover it contains enclosed drive; the illustration is based on a Rolls-Royce Phantom II Barker-bodied Pullman Limousine, constructed in 1929, by which date the open drive configuration had been all but deleted from coachbuilders' portfolios. The body closely resembles the saloon of the same period (see *Figure 1*), differing principally in length and, in this instance, the fact that the door panels have been deepened to cover the chassis frame. Note the use of spring bumpers, a windscreen vizor, matching side and headlamps, and a back panel turn-under almost as acute as on the foregoing body. In short, an archetypal large limousine of the late Vintage era.

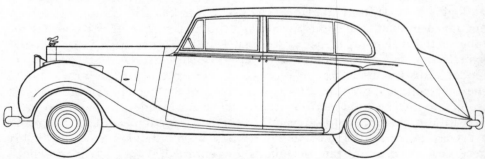

Figure 11 Rolls-Royce Silver Wraith Freestone & Webb Limousine, 1952

An interval of twenty-three years is a tremendous span of time when considering the progress of body styling, yet the 1952-vintage limousine shown in *Figure 11* is in several respects rather old-fashioned in comparison with other bodies of its age - reflecting perhaps the conservatism of coach-builders' clientele - notably forward of the front door: a centre-hinged bonnet, large exposed headlamp shells and very prominent front wings together with what appears at first glance to be a running-board, though it is in fact an outward extension of the door panels to complete the wing line.

110

The Freestone and Webb body is undeniably elegant and displays to advantage the typical sweeping lines of most English coachbuilt limousines of the 1950s. The chassis upon which this particular body was mounted, the Rolls-Royce Silver Wraith, was to some degree an awkward base on which to produce a well-balanced design containing the amount of interior space required of a limousine, since the wheelbase, even in its longest form, was a trifle short; in this body the rear occupants were placed behind the rear axle line as a consequence of this shortcoming.

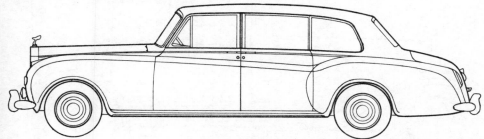

Figure 12 Rolls-Royce Phantom V Limousine, 1963

Finally, we arrive at the modern English limousine *(Figure 12)*, one that is currently in production on the Rolls-Royce Phantom VI chassis at the Willesden plant of H.J. Mulliner, Park Ward Ltd. The design originally made its debut under the aegis of Park Ward in 1959 on the Phantom V chassis, so that in reality the styling belongs to the late 1950s and is therefore not very much younger in terms of years than the previous body illustrated in *Figure 11*, in spite of which the overall shape is entirely dissimilar to the latter - a considerable percentage of the credit for which is owed to the much longer wheelbase of the later chassis. A wing line remains clearly evident in the sculptured side panels, the headlamps have been incorporated into the front panel alongside the instantly recognisable radiator shell, the passenger area has been increased quite dramatically and the long wheelbase has allowed the use of a very large boot in due proportion to the remainder of the body. The illustration is taken from a Phantom V Limousine of 1963, identified by one of the few outwardly detectable differences between the two models, namely the fitment on the Phantom VI of forward-hinged rear doors which the illustrated model clearly does not possess: note the door handles. Heavy bumpers and massive overriders are provided, commensurate with the near 20-foot bulk of the car, to complete the specification, and an important aspect is the very large window area, an absolute necessity in today's crowded traffic conditions.

4 Sedanca de Ville

As has already been stated, the sedanca de ville body style is no longer fashionable but is nonetheless included here because for the first

Automobile body design

twenty years of its forty-year existence the style was very popular - in terms of formal-bodied cars - and many sedancas de ville were influenced by a number of other body types, thereby creating most distinctive designs. A relatively small quantity of sedancas de ville were produced after World War II, and only a mere handful after 1960 by James Young of Bromley, the then sole remaining coachbuilder to offer such bodies; the last of the line was completed in 1965 *(Figure 16)*.

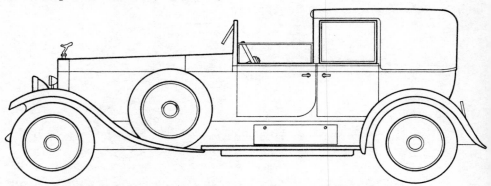

Figure 13 Rolls-Royce Phantom I Barker Sedanca de Ville, 1926

Figure 13 depicts a Barker-bodied Rolls-Royce Phantom I Sedanca de Ville of 1926, a body which correlates to the limousine style of that period (compare with *Figure 10)* apart from the very large blind rear quarter panels and of course the de ville front compartment; being of limousine proportions the rear compartment of this specimen could accommodate occasional seats with room to spare. Thus it is fair to say that until the early 1930s sedanca de ville bodies closely followed limousine design.

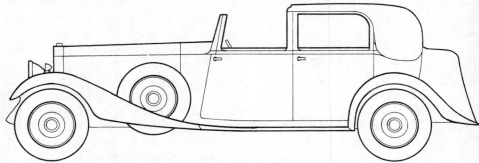

Figure 14 Rolls-Royce Phantom II Park Ward Sedanca de Ville, 1933

The next illustration, *Figure 14,* a 1933 Rolls-Royce Phantom II Park Ward Sedanca de Ville, shows the style beginning to break away from preponderantly limousine characteristics and crystallizing into a semi-touring format; the car evinces a cross-fertilization between a sports saloon, a touring

112

saloon and a limousine (the latter in regard to the large overall length of the body and use of a division). Note the enclosed boot, a large one too, in readiness for long-distance touring, and a relatively close-coupled passenger area which now does not really contain adequate space for occasional seating. Having stated that sedancas de ville of this era relinquished limousine styling, this statement must be retracted to some degree since for those applications where capacious rear compartments were particularly specified limousine-like lines were in fact retained (see illustration of Windovers body, Part II). In the austere 1930s a single car had to perform both formal and informal, ie touring, roles, whereas in the more carefree days of the 1920s separate cars would have been kept for specific roles; therefore a sedanca de ville tended towards an informality of line after the Vintage period, which confirmed its dual purpose.

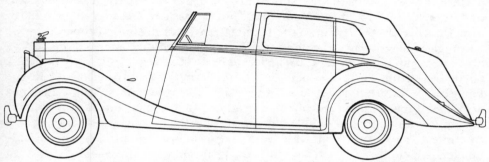

Figure 15 Rolls-Royce Silver Wraith H.J. Mulliner Sedanca de Ville, 1949

Post-war English sedancas de ville reverted back to the design policy of the 1920s by being styled in a similar vein to equivalent limousine bodywork; the majority were indeed simply modified limousines. This inter-body relationship is clearly portrayed on comparing a 1949 Sedanca de Ville *(Figure 15:* H.J. Mulliner-bodied Rolls-Royce Silver Wraith) with a limousine of approximately the same age *(Figure 11);* the bodies happen to emanate from two different coachworks but the lines are extremely alike and typify English formal body design of the 1940s and early 1950s. This particular sedanca de ville incorporates pillarless rear door lights, the window upright shown in the drawing being part of the frame of the opening rear quarter light.

The James Young Rolls-Royce Phantom V Sedanca de Ville, *Figure 16,* conforms precisely to the above rule in that it was adapted directly from its more widespread limousine counterpart. The illustrated model is in actuality the final sedanca de ville to be fabricated, and identified as so being by the shape of the rear quarter light, known as a 'Hooper' light after that coachbuilding firm whose symbol it was; the quarter lights of previous sedancas de ville and limousines of this James Young design were of rounded

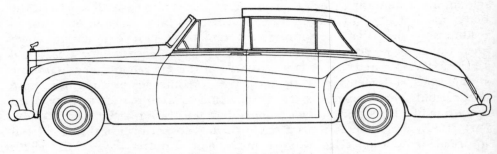

Figure 16 Rolls-Royce Phantom V James Young Sedanca de Ville, 1965

pattern, broadly akin to that shown in *Figure 15*. Before this final body was undertaken in 1965 James Young had not constructed a sedanca de ville for over three years, testifying to the terminal post-war decline of the body type - though it in no way reflected on the competence of James Young or any other leading coachbuilder to arrive at a satisfactory design. Although it emanated from the same period as the Park Ward-designed Rolls-Royce Phantom V Limousine, ie during the late 1950s, the James Young Sedanca de Ville retains a more traditional appearance than the latter car in respect of the more individually delineated front and rear wings and flowing tail treatment, nevertheless in the opinion of many present-day automobile fanciers - including the author - it is unsurpassed in its poise and elegance of line by any other formal body built in the past two decades. A fitting tribute to the last heir of a noble lineage.

5 Estate Car

The modern estate car traces its beginnings to private motor buses for conveyance of persons - servants, house guests, etc - to and from stations at a time when the railway system in this country was the prime method of long-distance travel. The uses to which successive (and concurrent) types of estate car were put are outlined in Part I, so it is not necessary to reitemise them at this juncture.

A representative wagonette, an early omnibus-type estate car derived from the horse-drawn wagonette, is exhibited in *Figure 17;* the chassis utilised for this particular body (a 40/50 hp Rolls-Royce) is quite unusual. A cranked windscreen of which the upper section may be folded down, is a common feature of Veteran and early Edwardian open cars, and the rear-entrance passenger compartment is shown here protected by a detachable waterproof cover (which we would nowadays call a tonneau cover). Except for this compartment the shape of the car is typical of an early open Silver Ghost Rolls-Royce, an expensive basis on which to mount a 'utility' body.

114

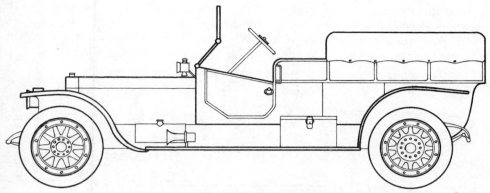

Figure 17 Rolls-Royce Silver Ghost Wagonette, 1907

Even though they were conventional fitments at the time, several items on this 1907 car are worthy of mention, notably the klaxon and toolbox affixed to the running-board, the tank containing calcium carbide crystals that, when mixed with water, generated acetylene gas for lighting the headlamps, and the artillery wheels (named after the heavy wooden spoked wheels fitted to pieces of ordnance), the rear wheel having a larger number of spokes and a broader hub than the front wheel to cope with both the sheer weight on the back axle and the braking action; front wheel brakes were some years away, so that the rear wheels took all the strain of braking this heavy car.

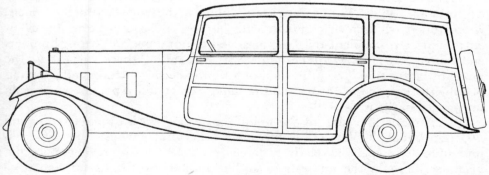

Figure 18 Rolls-Royce 25/30 Estate Car, 1937

The estate car of thirty years later was a very different proposition to the wagonette; apart from the overall development of chassis and body design in the intervening period the car is now totally closed and presents a somewhat van-like appearance. From the rear door forward the car is identical to a saloon, but the roof is extended rearwards from the rear door and a tall back panel containing either a door or a drop-down tailgate conceals a considerable volume of space for load-carrying. The 1937 Rolls-

Automobile body design

Royce 25/30 depicted in *Figure 18* has an externally timber-framed body panelled in sheet metal, the normal method of estate car construction extant until well after the Second World War, and it also sports a spare wheel attached to the door/tailgate - deformable stern protection, no less.

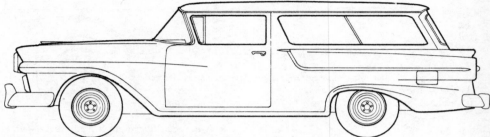

Figure 19 Ford Ranch Wagon, 1957

The mid-1950s is the next logical stage in the progress of estate car design; we look to the United States to supply an example of the all-metal 'wagon' based on a saloon structure and built to saloon standards of comfort which, akin to a previous stage in estate car history, was pioneered by American motor manufacturers. The car illustrated in *Figure 19* is a 1957 Ford Ranch Wagon, a mass-produced body (unlike the previous two examples of estate car bodywork) in which the wing panels, doors, bonnet, windscreen and secondary external fittings were common to a variety of body types within the Ford range of that year, the differences between the types being confined to the upper body structure alone. The styling is archetypal mid-1950's American: bulbous heavily-sculptured panels, wrap-around windscreen complete with 'dog-leg' pillar that jarred knees on entry and exit, incipient tail fins, massive but not especially strong bumpers and above all, lashings of chrome. Notwithstanding these vulgarities, the mode of fabrication - the utilisation of as few exclusive fixtures and panels as possible to keep costs down - and the fundamental design parameters remain unchanged in the mid-1970s.

A modern version of the ubiquitous estate car is displayed in *Figure 20,* the Vauxhall Victor FE introduced in 1972. Whilst the design is undoubtedly shapely a relatively large amount of load-carrying space has been sacrificed in the interests of styling fashion by the use of a sharply-angled rear panel, an indication of the current estate car philosophy adhered to by an increasing number of manufacturers which demands that the maximum possible load volume available within any given set of body dimensions be allied and/or offset in design and execution against the 'fastback' line so much in vogue at the present time. Several features of this Vauxhall bear noting: firstly, there is no longer any suggestion whatsoever of wing contours in the old-fashioned sense, secondly the provision of very slim, close-fitting bumpers that do little to render the front or rear of the car

116

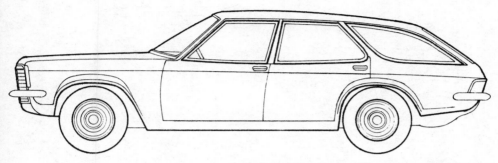

Figure 20 Vauxhall Victor FE Estate Car, 1972

invulnerable, and thirdly, and most importantly, the huge window area which, in combination with slender pillars, offers remarkably good all-round visibility for the car's occupants.

6 Saloon Coupe

Although this term was utilised by merely a small number of English coachbuilders and only over a period of some fifteen years from 1935 or thereabouts, saloon coupe nonetheless provides a succinct title for application to any two-door close-coupled foursome sporting saloon, of which many examples have been manufactured in the past forty-five years, and of which a certain number continue to appear in current listings. In the modern context a saloon coupe cannot easily be differentiated from the popular four-seater coupe style, therefore I have formulated a criterion for employment of the title: to qualify as a saloon coupe a two-door, four-light closed body of quasi-coupe styling should possess a passenger area of sufficient capacity to house four people in the same levels of comfort and spaciousness as an orthodox saloon of similar external proportions. This definitive rule thus immediately discounts very close-coupled sports coupes of the BMW 3.0 CS and Alfa Romeo 2000 GTV genre.

Turning to *Figure 21,* we see a coachbuilt two-door sporting saloon of interesting, if not especially elegant or imposing appearance, from the very late Vintage period when general body design was evolving towards softer, less severe outlines through the use of larger-radius curves and de-emphasis of the vertical, culminating in the sweeping lines of the mid to late 1930s, before the reconstitution of design philosophy after World War II promoted full-width bodies, gradual disappearance of wings and incorporation of headlamps into the front panel. This particular example, a 1930 Gurney Nutting Rolls-Royce 20/25, exudes a certain charm; the wings are the most striking feature of the vehicle, the forward extension of the rear wing (doubling as a running-board) sweeps towards but does not quite reach the beautifully shaped front wing, terminating just below and to the aft of the

117

Figure 21 Rolls-Royce 20/25 Gurney Nutting Saloon Coupe, 1930

side-mounted spare wheel. The sloping windscreen, capped by a vizor, and the enclosed boot further testify to the car's appeal to the sporting yet discerning customer. This pleasant, unspectacular design grows upon acquaintance.

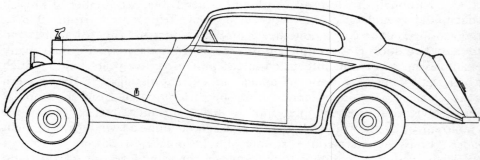

Figure 22 Rolls-Royce 25/30 Gurney Nutting Saloon Coupe, 1937

Another Gurney Nutting design is illustrated in *Figure 22,* a Rolls-Royce 25/30 Saloon Coupe; in common with the previous (and subsequent) mid-1930s bodies illustrated here in Part III, the tremendous upsurge of design development realised during that period is patently obvious when this 1937 model is contrasted against its predecessor. Gone is the somewhat 'dumpy' appearance, to be replaced by a superbly sleek outline emphasised by the downswept waistline which is duplicated in the frame of the pillarless side windows, the whole highlighted by the voluptuous wings. By any standard an exemplary body, a complement to both the ingenuity of the coachbuilder and the discernment of the fortunate owner.

In spite of the fact that a very considerable quantity of standard saloons were turned out in the ten-year model tenure of the Rolls-Royce factory at Crewe from 1955, only a minor percentage of Silver Cloud chassis were allocated to coachbuilders for fitment of special bodies, and of those

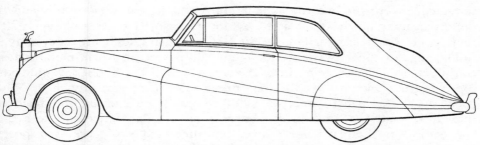

Figure 23 Rolls-Royce Silver Cloud I Freestone & Webb Two-Door Saloon, 1956

the most numerous were the celebrated H.J. Mulliner Drop-Head Coupes (see 8 Drop-Head Coupe; *Figure 26*). In 1956 the eminent coachbuilders Freestone and Webb constructed a handsome two-door saloon body on an early Silver Cloud frame *(Figure 23)*, instigated by a previous four-door saloon body that had been designed to suit Silver Wraith and Silver Dawn chassis; the car was simply called a two-door saloon by its creators, though the term saloon coupe is perfectly apt as an alternative designation. This car's curvilinear profile, which is characterised by a downswept, body-length elongation of the front wing without a suspicion of a rear wing structure - to introduce such would utterly destroy the lines - typifies the approach followed by Freestone and Webb and Hooper to semi-formal body design during the 1950s, resulting in some exceptionally fine shapes of which this example is near paramount. Advantage has been taken of full body sides to stress the streamlined aspect through the use of harmonious wing and waistline swaging, the effect being reinforced by the manner in which the roof-, boot- and wing-lines are contrived to conjoin at rear bumper level.

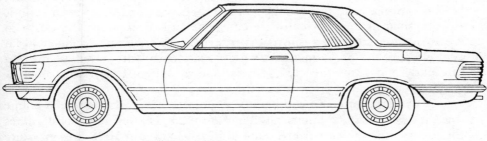

Figure 24 Mercedes-Benz 350SLC, 1972

A contemporary saloon coupe is depicted in *Figure 24,* the Mercedes-Benz 350SLC, which was initially unveiled before an admiring public in 1972. Fundamentally a stretched 350SL, the two-seater sporting model of the Mercedes-Benz range, this car sets out to and succeeds in providing ample seating for four; it could also be styled a hardtop saloon coupe since the pillarless side windows are all capable of being fully retracted, except the hardtop appellation is no longer utilised on this side of the Atlantic as much as formerly. As in the majority of cars of the 1970s there is no wingline as such on the 350SLC, the slab sides being relieved by a full-length horizontal waistline moulding and protective bright-metal strips, containing rubber inserts, between the wheel arches. The 350SLC exhibits its sports-touring ancestry via the long bonnet and comparatively short boot deck; the slatted panel within the side window frame is an unusual feature, though if truth be told its presence is merely decorative, whereas the corrugations in the rear lamp lens on the other hand serve a useful purpose: the maintenance of a reasonable level of illumination in muddy or dusty conditions by increasing the effective area of the lens. The 350SLC, together with its outwardly identical sister the 450SLC - furnished with a 4½-litre powerplant in lieu of the 3½-litre of the 350SLC - is indeed a veritable saloon coupe in the modern idiom.

7 Fixed-Head Coupe

Since the designation 'drop-head coupe' has been irrevocably displaced in favour of the quasi-Transatlantic 'convertible' over the past decade or so the titular differentiation between open and closed coupes, ie drop-head and fixed-head, has become increasingly irrelevant, so much so that the term coupe in contemporary parlance automatically implies a closed body style. However, fixed-head coupe remains the generic term for all closed coupe bodies, whatever the type or size; the very wide field of choice resulting therefrom presents something of a problem when confronted with the task of selecting a cross-section of such styles over four decades. The fact that the 1939-45 War marked a watershed in univeral automotive design must by this stage have become reasonably evident from the foregoing text and illustrations, and is perhaps more apparent in fixed-head coupe bodywork than in the types already considered thus far, since the post-war coupe is substantially more sports-orientated in external appearance and far more aggressive in performance than its frequently rather sedate pre-war counterpart, and consequently tends to appeal to a different sector of the car-buying market.

A characteristic and comparatively popular form of fixed-head coupe of the Vintage years is demonstrated in *Figure 25*. The severely angular lines of this two-seater three-quarter coupe built by Barker in 1928 present quite a sizable frontal area to be forced through the airstream - a feature of most Vintage bodies - which in combination with the not over-generously powered Rolls-Royce Twenty chassis conspired to render a less than sparkling performance. Nevertheless the body is patently honest in its simplicity and dearth of unnecessary adornment; what it may lack in superficial 'elan' it ultimately gains in being fabricated and appointed to the very high standards of craftsmanship associated with the name of Barker. When opened, the back

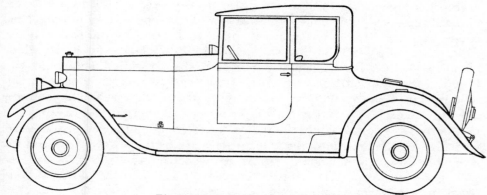

Figure 25 Rolls-Royce 20 Barker Three-Quarter Coupe, 1928

of the dickey seat corresponds with the angle of the backward-tilted spare wheel (the presence of the former is indicated in the illustration by a grab-handle on the tail deck and a small step-plate on top of the rear wing); an upright or forward-tilted wheel mounting would at least seriously restrict and at most nullify the fitment of such a seat. In any event, the occupants of the dickey seat in this particular body presumably felt pretty remote from the driver and their enjoyment of a journey rapidly reduced to unrelieved monotony due to entire lack of forward vision, brought about by the broad expanse of the back panel, and assuaged only by the regulation miniscule rear window - two good reasons why dickey seats were more commonly to be found on open bodies.

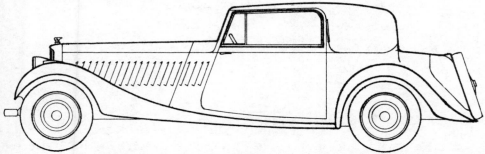

Figure 26 Bentley 4¼-litre Freestone & Webb Fixed-Head Coupe, 1937

The next example of a fixed-head coupe is a Freestone and Webb design on a 1937 4¼-litre Bentley chassis *(Figure 26)*. The immediate impression gained relative to the older Barker body is of increased length and reduced height, the latter aspect principally due to the longer passenger area profile. In common with the 1928 car the outline and general arrangement of this design lends itself to construction in the alternative drop-head form, indeed many instances of drop-head coupe bodies from the mid-1920s to the

121

Automobile body design

outbreak of war in 1939 were indistinguishable, when their hoods were raised, from fixed-heads and vice versa. The Freestone and Webb fixed-head coupe, otherwise coupe limousine since it is also a four-seater body, conforms to the 1930's 'English orthodox' approach to design in which blandness and aesthetic sensibility held sway over frenetic flamboyance and frivolity, the latter attributes (positive or negative, depending on one's point of view) customarily addictive to a number of French coachbuilders simply did not appeal to the discriminating Briton of the period. Two features of the body are noteworthy; firstly the exposed tail-mounted spare wheel partially countersunk into the boot panel, a transitional stage between the venerable fully-exposed side or rear-rigged wheel and the later fully-enclosed variety. Moisture and dirt trapped between the tyre and the indented body panel must have posed something of a problem on this car. Secondly, the large blind rear quarter panel, a major component in the overall appearance of the car, may have been entirely compatible with traffic conditions in 1937, but it could not be reconciled with the overcrowded motoring conditions of forty years later when all-round visibility is a vital safety factor - notwithstanding which all too many current motor cars are blinkered by unwieldy rear quarters, and when one considers that by and large their immediate predecessors were noted for 'greenhouse' superstructures it becomes abundantly plain that sound common sense has yielded to stylistic caprice; an irrational state of affairs, without doubt.

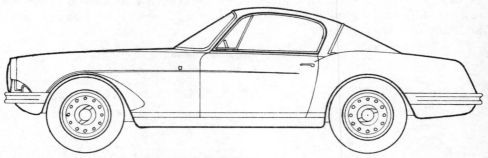

Figure 27 Jaguar XK150 Bertone Coupe, 1958

No such criticism need be levelled at the one-off body created around Jaguar XK150 mechanicals by the Italian coachbuilder Bertone in 1958, shown in *Figure 27*. Strictly a two-seater of *Gran Turismo* character this car's outline typifies the European sports coupe of the mid-1950s onwards, of which Ferrari, Maserati, Aston Martin, Fiat and Volvo amongst others were exponents. A hint of a rear wing is given by the upraised line above the rear wheel arch, whilst a front wing-line is intimated by the roll-over of the wing panel onto the bonnet deck, together with a protuberant headlamp assembly physically detached from the front panel. The deep windscreen and substantial wrap-around rear window greatly assist in the provision of excellent visibility from within the cockpit, a particularly important feature for a low-slung car such as this as comparative lack of height creates its own problems in traffic. The fortunate owner would find parking a simple task for all four corners, bounded by the headlamp rims and rear wing tips, are clearly visible from the driving seat.

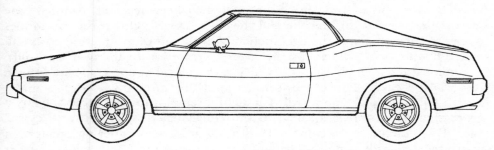

Figure 28 American Motors Javelin, 1973

A recent fixed-head coupe is represented by the 1973-model American Motors Javelin *(Figure 28),* a car of considerable performance potential and quintessentially Transatlantic design. The most striking feature on first acquaintance with the Javelin is its very long front overhang (the distance from the front wheel centre to the forward edge of the bumper), especially when compared with very much smaller rear overhang. Surprisingly enough at this contemporary stage of design progression, simulated wings are apparent in the form of heavily sculptured panelling above the wheels; though embryonic in nature they are nevertheless a fairly dominant feature of the design, contributing in large measure to the attainment of a deliberately 'muscular' look intended to denote enormous power. Pillarless side window construction is utilised and the interior seating is very close-coupled; the rear window is mounted at approximately the same angle as the trailing edge of the side-window frame and is inset between rear-swept 'sails' or 'dorsal fins', extensions of the roofline on either side of the body. The rear window cannot therefore be seen in the illustration, being a side view, but it does give a clue as to how much rear vision is available: combined with the tall rear panel (higher than the bonnet line) the visibility rearwards leaves a great deal to be desired. This feature apart, the window area is commensurate with that expected in modern vehicles.

The overall arrangement of most latter-day fixed-head coupes, as opposed to saloon coupes and pre-war fixed-head coupes, falls down in one major respect, that is, the highly restricted or non-existent rear seating which renders the style impracticable for a variety of applications where seating capacity is at a premium.

Automobile body design

8 Drop-Head Coupe

The designation drop-head coupe is analogous to fixed-head coupe in that definitively it remains the collective term for four-seater open cars, albeit rarely recognised as such nowadays after its eclipse in contemporary bodywork nomenclature by the synonymous designation convertible, itself a corruption of the American term convertible coupe. The drop-head coupe's pre-war popularity began to wane at an increasingly rapid rate after 1945, until by the end of the 1960s the nadir had been reached. Amongst the factors that caused this decline and the shift towards closed cars by former open-car adherents was the ever-increasing inflation of production costs and hence retail prices (which rose in inverse proportion to the numbers sold), the comparative simplicity with which a drop-head coupe could be broken into via the easily-slashed fabric hood, and the antipathy towards family-sized cars fitted with supposedly 'draughty, flapping hoods' occasioned by a generation of motorists attuned to the convenience and solidity of closed cars. These factors were compounded by policies of product rationalisation instituted by leading motor manufacturers during the 1960s which further depleted the then minute production level of drop-head coupes, leaving a handful of hand-crafted, highly expensive convertibles to carry on the tradition.

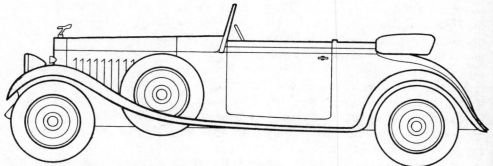

Figure 29 Rolls-Royce Phantom II Carlton Drop-Head Coupe, 1930

The 1930 Rolls-Royce Phantom II Drop-Head Coupe crafted by the Carlton Carriage Company, illustrated in *Figure 29* is an instance of the intermediate stage in body design between the earlier tall, square-cut styles and the smoother lines of later years; the body is an amalgam of both these principles. The wing profile demonstrates incipiently flowing contours in comparison with that of the 1928 Barker Fixed-Head Coupe shown in *Figure 25*, yet the body proper tends towards an approximate facsimile of the latter, though the larger foursome passenger area together with the space over the tail deck reserved for accommodation of the folded hood framework precludes the fitment of a dickey seat - not that this would be necessary in a four-seater body. The quarter light retracts flush with the

124

bodyside, in common with the action of the door window, in order to enable the detachable pillar between the windows, which abuts against the cant rails (these constitute part of the hood frame), to be removed on folding the hood, thereby achieving an entirely unobstructed superstructure, the clean lines of which are broken only by the stubby pillar attachment socket. In sum, a car that is pleasing to the eye without displaying any outstandingly outre features: a simple, well-proportioned and very English design.

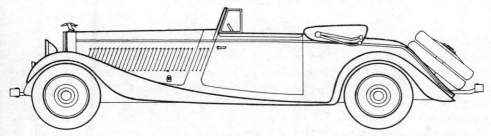

Figure 30 Hispano-Suiza V12 Drop-Head Coupe, c.1936

Figure 30 depicts a V-12 Hispano-Suiza fitted with a two-light drop-head coupe bodywork by an unknown but probably English coachbuilder, around the year 1936. The outline is sleeker than the Carlton-bodied Rolls-Royce of six years earlier - due in part to the longer wheelbase - and a sporting role is envisaged by the inclusion of a long row of angled louvres ranged along the bonnet and scuttle sides, in combination with a relatively low windscreen and truncated tail dominated by a pair of rakishly-mounted spare wheels. Spring bumpers make a welcome re-appearance here, the rear bumper being mounted well aft of the twin spares on commensurately lengthy struts, and the provision of a front quarter light at this early juncture is a notable feature. The tail treatment is a mite unfortunate in respect of the abrupt change in direction of the prominent waistline moulding; the side aspect would benefit from a more gradually sloping moulding in greater harmony with the slope of the rear wing, even though this modification might result in a miniscule reduction in the impression of immense bodily length, imparted to a considerable degree by this moulding. However, the appearance of the car is altogether quite striking, yet one feels that this particular body would perhaps have been better suited to a somewhat shorter chassis, an opinion borne out by the fact that the wings seem a trifle slender, relative to the broad expanse of the side panelling.

The third example of a drop-head coupe *(Figure 31)* is a familiar shape to aficionados of the automobile, namely the Silver Cloud Rolls-Royce bodied by H.J. Mulliner, subsequently H.J. Mulliner-Park Ward. This magnificent motor car had a total production life of over five years from 1960, during which time a comparatively large number were built - bearing

125

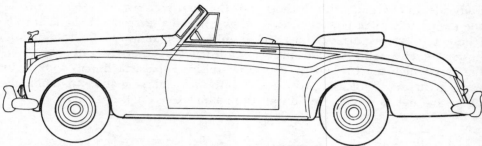

Figure 31 Rolls-Royce Silver Cloud II H.J. Mulliner Drop-Head Coupe, 1960

in mind the very low level of general coachbuilding activity at that time - and was identical in all mechanical and bodily respects to the factory-manufactured saloon, bar the replacement of four doors by two large ones, plus of course the (power-operated) folding hood complete with the individual four-light side window arrangement necessitated by the structural revision concomitant upon the drop-head style. The distinctive swept wings, tall boot line and equally tall longitudinally-hinged bonnet - vestiges of former design philosophies - combine to convey an impression of timeless elegance intermingled with stately panache. An expression that positively underlines the excellence of design (owing in this instance to Rolls-Royce's own design staff) and execution for which English coachbuilders have always been justly renowned.

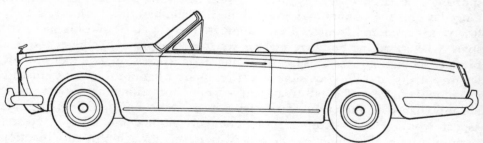

Figure 32 Rolls-Royce Corniche Convertible, 1971

The successor to the Silver Cloud Drop-Head Coupe from H.J. Mulliner-Park Ward is the current Rolls-Royce Corniche Convertible *(Figure 32)* that made its debut in 1971 and for which there is a waiting list of prospective purchasers several years long, despite being amongst the world's most expensive cars; it is assuredly one of the most coveted. Derived from the Silver Shadow Saloon whose shape it resembles, though not so exactly as its predecessor with the then current Silver Cloud Saloon, and using basically the same mechanical components as its Crewe-built cousin, the Corniche is a longer, lower and more fleet-looking car than the Silver Cloud Drop-Head Coupe - indeed its performance corroborates this impression - and conforms to modern notions of design in its somewhat 'boxy' outline, relieved by sculptured panels and an intimation of a wing-line; were it not for the dip in the lines just aft of the door the profile would be flat and uninteresting. Mark the lower radiator shell and bonnet line and the very much more substantial windscreen, features that aid forward visibility, compared with its forerunner. Very much the essence of modernity in compatible juxtaposition with the ancient and maintained standards of coachcraft, the Corniche Convertible is more than able to stand comparison in appointment and execution with any other motor car manufactured today or in the past.

9 Cabriolet

Insofar as this study of styling evolution is concerned a cabriolet is implicitly the Anglicized, four-door interpretation of the body type and not the Continental cabriolet which, as explained in Part I, is generally synonymous with our drop-head coupe or convertible. Therefore wherever the term appears hereunder the four-door format is inferred unless otherwise stated.

The halcyon days of the archetypal English cabriolet were undoubtedly the 1920s; the type originally arose in the Edwardian era as a formal chauffeured carriage, and thereafter was constructed for both formal usage and as a refined tourer for the owner-driver until the tide of saloon styles began to overwhelm the old-established configurations at the close of the 1920s. The upshot of this motoring revolution was that orders for four-door cabriolets plummetted drastically, yet the type, continuously adapted to conform with prevailing fashions, remained firmly lodged in coachbuilders' manifestos and a number of mass-produced examples were listed right up till the spread of war in 1939. The first ten years after recommencement of motor manufacturing in 1945-6 saw the final and irrevocable disappearance of the cabriolet in the United Kingdom; merely some half-dozen individually-designed bodies on Daimler and Rolls-Royce chassis were constructed in that period. Daimler-Benz AG of Stuttgart, West Germany, had nonetheless found a market for such cabriolets, albeit small, during the early 1950s and met the challenge with their Mercedes-Benz 300; this was the body type's European swansong. In 1961 however, the American Ford Motor Company introduced a four-door convertible coupe version of their prestigious Lincoln Continental, a cabriolet in all but name. The model remained in fairly limited production - by Transatlantic standards - for six years, during which time only a handful were exported to Europe and the British Isles. Its demise in 1967 marked the veritable end of the style.

The body illustrated in *Figure 33* exemplifies the cabriolet style of the Vintage era. In the open state it is more or less identical to a conventional flush-sided touring body, and for this reason was called a torpedo cabriolet by its creators, the London firm of Barker, who mounted the body on a Rolls-Royce Phantom I (or New Phantom, as it was then

127

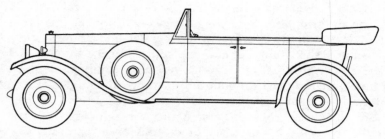

Figure 33 Rolls-Royce Phantom I Barker Torpedo Cabriolet, 1925

known) chassis in 1925. Unlike a straightforward tourer of the period which was furnished with sidescreens, this torpedo cabriolet possessed retracting glass side windows - three per side and therefore of six-light format - together with a tight-fitting hood for the really effective weather protection expected in this class of motor car; the window frame pillars hinged downwards on collapsing the hood to accentuate the already clean lines of the design. Note the separate wings sandwiched by a plain running-board (the advent of running-boards styled as part of the front wing line had not yet arrived), the orthodox folding luggage grid at the tail of the car and the matching side and headlamps. A sloping windscreen was seldom seen in 1925; the specimen depicted here is particularly interesting in that it incorporates flanking triangular side windows which plug the gap between the windscreen and the front door window frame as a further weather-protective measure, a device which is not only effective from this aspect but also as an enhancement of the overall body style. This Barker cabriolet exudes a majestic air which is nevertheless subtly compounded by a somewhat 'sporting' mien, testimony to the coachbuilder's competence in creating a design suitable for all occasions.

Even before their infamous assumption of power in Germany in 1933, senior members of the Nazi hierarchy had developed a taste for large cabriolet motor cars, to which indigenous manufacturers such as Horch, Maybach and especially Daimler-Benz catered accordingly. These cabriolets grew ever vaster in size and weight as the 1930s wore on, and the acknowledged supremo amongst these cars was without a shadow of doubt the immense Grosser Mercedes-Benz, which had initially been unveiled in 1930 and underwent several mechanical and structural mutations throughout its ten-year production life. The example portrayed in *Figure 34* is a 1939 six-light eight-seater cabriolet (called the cabriolet 'F' by the manufacturers) powered by a 7.7-litre supercharged engine that could thrust the twenty-foot body along the road at a considerable rate, although the optional bullet-proof, armour-plated version penalised the performance since the power unit had then to cope with a seven-ton bulk. The Grosser ('Great') Mercedes-Benz was aptly named! Everything about the body is massive yet

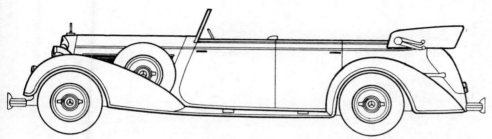

Figure 34 Grosser Mercedes-Benz Cabriolet 'F', 1939

well-proportioned, a trait that characterised the larger models of the marque from the supercharged Porsche designs of the mid to late 1920s right through until 1954, when the separate-wing style was updated and slab-sided Mercedes models were introduced for the first time; the Mercedes-Benz range in the first post-war decade comprised distinctly old-fashioned styles, being based to a large extent on pre-war designs.

Turning to specifics anent the Grosser model, the wings, connected by a sill rib upon which are placed step-plates, are heavy yet perfectly shaped, the bulbous tail contributes in no small measure to the impressive substantiality of the body, the bumpers are outrigged well beyond the body for really effective protection of the latter (the disadvantage of this arrangement being that the already formidable length of the vehicle is palpably intensified) and the pressed-steel disc wheels are located by king-sized knock-off hub caps. All in all, judged on its own merits, this is a colossal motor car containing styling features that taken individually are ponderous in execution but in coalition produce a purposeful, commanding appearance; however, many people still experience difficulty in attempting to divorce appreciation of the Grosser's aesthetic propensities from its original, well-documented role as a mobile platform for that swastika-bedecked megalomaniac and his minions of yesteryear.

An altogether more graceful cabriolet is that designed and fabricated by Hooper in 1952 for the celebrated financier Nubar Gulbenkian (*Figure 35*). One of the last English four-door cabriolets, this special body was mounted on a Rolls-Royce Silver Wraith chassis; in common with the Freestone and Webb Saloon Coupe of four years later (see *Figure 23*) the large front wings are extended rearwards in a gradually sloping line to terminate aft of the rear wheels, without the slightest suggestion of a rear wing, and harmonising with the waistline mouldings to emphasise the sleek profile of the car. The sculpted line running from the upper forward edge of the front door downwards across the rear door and wheel spat effectively relieves what would otherwise be an overbearing expanse of plain panelling. The folding hood is power-operated and when lowered is encapsulated beneath a flush-fitting metal cover behind the rear seats, a very neat

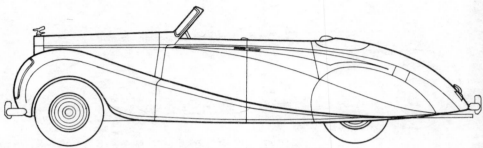

Figure 35 Rolls-Royce Silver Wraith Hooper Cabriolet, 1952

arrangement which complements the clean body lines and aids rearward vision, in total contrast to the prominent masses of exposed, collapsed hood fabric and framework evident on the earlier cabriolets illustrated here. The head and auxiliary lamps are mounted behind a transparent cover comprising the leading face of the front wing, a configuration conducive to an exceptionally smooth appearance which was initially utilised on the first of the famous 'Docker Daimlers', the individualistic extravaganzas constructed in the 1950s during the chairmanship and influence of Sir Bernard and Lady Docker in the Daimler-owning (at that time) BSA Group. Mr Gulbenkian's cabriolet was used by HM Queen Elizabeth in the course of the Royal visit to Nigeria in 1956.

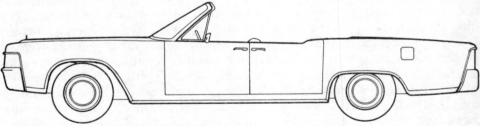

Figure 36 Lincoln Continental, 1965

A perusal of progress in cabriolet design would not be complete without a glance at the last of the breed, the Lincoln Continental, a 1965 version of which is depicted in *Figure 36*, (though not so called by the manufacturers, for the purposes of this survey the model shall be termed a cabriolet). The sizable dimensions - unwieldy to modern European eyes - bonnet and boot decks very long in relation to the passenger area and deep bumpers, mark the Continental as a Transatlantic creation; the side panels are conspicuous by the lack of relief or adornment excepting delineation by a plated strip that follows the base line and wheel arches of the body. Perhaps the ultimate in slab-sided styling. Were it not for the 'kink' in the upper body line the profile would prove pretty uninspiring. Even as late as 1965, when thoughts and actions on the subject of vehicular safety were by no means dormant, rear-hinged rear doors were still being fitted to both sedan and cabriolet Continentals; by that time the anachronistic wrap-around windscreen so much in vogue in the 1950s had long since become an unrevered memory, and consequently the Continental sports a sensibly-shaped, very deep screen. The Continental differs from previous cabriolets in its very sophisticated mechanical specification and wealth of modern conveniences, being therefore a comfortable and rapid cabriolet which cannot however aspire to the poise and polish inherent in its distinguished antecedents.

10 Open Sports

The concluding body type in this dissertation is the sports car, which as previously indicated in Part I presents a predicament when confronted with the task of conjuring up an elucidative definition. However I have selected four models representing four successive and distinct styling phases; all are open two-seaters (bar one, a very occasional four-seater) which comply with the generally accepted principles of a sports car: good performance, tenacious roadholding, crisp handling and 'seat-of-the-pants' ride characteristics packaged in bodies of correspondingly evocative appearance.

The open sports car as we have known it since the mid-1920s owes much of its lineage to the light touring car of earlier times, whose relatively good handling countered by lamentable performance rendered it ripe for modification by insertion of higher-output power units. Such modified cars were for instance the small sports Salmsons and Amilcars. Allegiance was also owed to the comparatively cumbersome but much speedier and more reliable open tourer of the 3-litre Bentley and 30/98 Vauxhall genre, and a fruitful alliance of reliability, performance and handling brought forth the archetypal compact sports car towards the end of the Vintage era and throughout the 1930s: Frazer Nash, Bugatti, MG, Riley, the exclusive 1½-litre 'blown' (supercharged) Squire and the elusive Vale amongst a horde of sports-orientated marques of greater or lesser celebrity.

The Second World War was as much a turning-point in sports car design as in other body types; the old-style separate-wing format was adapted and eventually replaced by a fluid configuration of which the Farina-bodied Cisitalia and the Jaguar XK120 were prime instigators. MG set the trend for small sports cars in the United States with the highly successful TC model, Ferrari entered the fray with a twelve-cylinder spider, the Type 212, swiftly following it up with a succession of ever more astonishingly rapid V-12 cars, and Lotus commenced to release a stream of aerodynamically efficient two-seaters; however the 1960s saw many erstwhile sports cars take on a mellower aspect, frequently crystallizing into closed gran turismo cars of inflated size and avoirdupois and much enhanced price.

Open sports cars have become progressively more comfortable and   131

Automobile body design

amenable in the past fifteen years. Sidescreens and draughty detachable hoods have yielded to winding glass windows and snug folding hoods, such former luxuries as heaters and pile carpets are commonplace - ancillaries which would nowadays be remarkable by their absence - and the heavy, difficult-to-clean knock-on spoked wheels, previously de rigueur for sporting models long after their demise as standard fittings on other body types, have almost entirely disappeared in the face of competition from lightweight alloy wheels that require little maintenance. In sum, modern sports cars are more sybaritic and certainly less noisy than their exiguous forerunners, though whether they transmit a comparable sporting 'image' is open to question.

Figure 37 Frazer Nash TT Replica, 1933

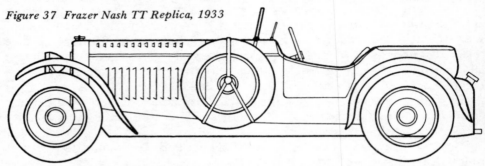

A sports car that varied little in basic design throughout its production existence of some fourteen years up till 1939 was the inimitable 'Chain Gang' Frazer Nash, so called because of the chain-drive transmission arrangement. The example illustrated in *Figure 37* is a 1933 TT Replica model (for edification of the cognoscenti, this is the six-cylinder Blackburne-engined version), the name commemorating Frazer Nash entries in sundry Tourist Trophy races during the early 1930s. The model does in fact possess a small rear seat which was normally protected by a tonneau cover; a full-length hood was an optional extra. The stark profile typifies sports car design of the late Vintage period and early 1930s; the functional wings match the uncomplicated body, which incorporates a comprehensively louvred bonnet, tub-like tail and a cutaway door - the body was so narrow that shoulder-room was at a premium and the cutaway was conveniently placed to enable the passenger's left arm to obtrude beyond the confines of the body; the gearlever and handbrake were also situated outboard because of the space restriction, which made the offside (ie driver's) cutaway doubly necessary. Some very small sports bodies were even narrower, so that the passenger's seat had to be 'staggered', ie set slightly aft of the driver's seat, in order to physically accommodate two average-sized people. The Frazer Nash's fuel tank is mounted at the extreme rear of the body, a highly vulnerable but typically Vintage location. The side-mounted spare wheel is held in place by leather straps, and twin aero screens are furnished in addition

132

to a full-width, fold-flat windscreen. An unpretentious but characterful sports car, which after the passage of forty-odd years still stands high in the ranks of those cars able to give positive pleasure in motoring by way of innate driveability.

Figure 38 BMW 328, 1938

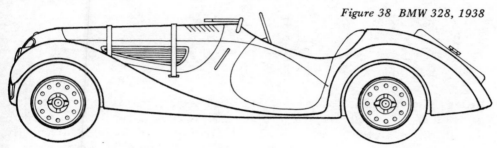

The next generation of sports cars was presaged by the German BMW (Bayerische Motoren Werke, ie Bavarian Motor Works) company in 1933 with the announcement of a drop-head coupe of precociously flowing lines. This theme was expanded by further models and in 1936 the renowned BMW 328 was unveiled, of which a 1938 version is shown in *Figure 38;* the fundamental lines of the original drop-head coupe were carried forward in only slightly modified form for the 328, comprising an all but full-width body, wings which were no longer separate entities from the body shell, headlamps fared into the valances that joined front wings to body, and a radiator concealed behind a rounded nose pierced by two narrow vertical grilles. The semi-streamlined shape enabled a fairly small-capacity (2-litre) engine to be used, giving the car a turn of speed considerably higher than its immediate competitors. Earlier examples of the 328 sported rear wheel spats, which were usually permanently removed by purchasers; cutaway doors and a centrally-split, fold-flat windscreen - without aero screens - were provided, and the spare wheel is neatly countersunk into the curvaceous tail. Of altogether different appearance than the foregoing Frazer Nash, the 328 foreshadowed the styling of post-war sports cars and was deservedly popular in Britain and Continental Europe.

The world-famous Jaguar XK120, portrayed in *Figure 39,* was released before a spell-bound public in the autumn of 1948. Owing nothing to any previous body shape, excepting perhaps in small but succinct measure to the BMW 328, the XK120 was justly hailed as a revolutionary concept in sports car design, setting the style for the ensuing thirteen years till the advent of the equally revolutionary E-type from the same stable in 1961. The lines are beautifully smooth and subtly rounded, the wings - very much part of the body structure - blending with and accentuating the long bonnet (enclosing a 3.4-litre power plant) and the slim swept tail. No frills are necessary, indeed the shape would be badly marred by addition of such

133

Figure 39 Jaguar XK120, 1948

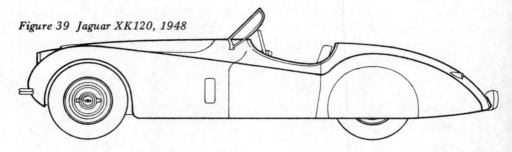

fittings as plated strips or louvres. The windscreen is permanently affixed, ie it cannot fold flat, and the customary cutaway cockpit side is still provided, though this is no longer an indispensable item since the body is sufficiently ample to accommodate two people with ease. Celluloid sidescreens and a detachable hood were furnished with the car, though, as with so many sports cars, the visually exciting impact of the profile was altered to the worse when these were fastened in place. The headlamps are mounted in prominent fairings in the valances flanking a small elliptical radiator grille, and rear wheel spats were standard fitments which (unlike those on a BMW 328) underline the cleanness of the outline; when knock-on spoked wheels were specified (these were made available fairly late in the XK120's six-year career) the spats were deleted, due to the protuberance of the eared hub caps attendant upon this option.

The XK120 Jaguar was and remains one of the outstanding designs of all time. It wielded a tremendous influence not only over subsequent Jaguar creations - see *Figures 7 and 8* - but also over products of motor industries throughout the world, the kudos for which the Jaguar Company can be justifiably proud.

The ultimate example of a sports car is the Spider variant of the prestigious Ferrari 365 GT/4, better known as the Daytona *(Figure 40)*. Styled by Pininfarina in 1969 and constructed in strictly limited quantities up till mid-1974 by Scaglietti, the Daytona Spider, which is little-known outside its native Italy, is almost identical bar the superstructure and rear deck line to its more widespread progenitor, the Daytona 'Berlinetta'. One of the fastest and most powerful production cars ever built, with a top speed in excess of 175 mph, the Daytona is a sports car in the grand manner. Every modern convenience is provided - no such crudities as sidescreens or awkward-to-erect hood - and the purposeful contours bespeak the tremendous performance potential; the low prow rises up towards the steeply raked windscreen, the body line dips a shade at the door and continues rearwards to the sharply truncated tail panel: factors that unite to render an aerodynamically sound body. The headlamps are concealed when not in use, being mounted in flush-fitting pods in the nose that are elevated

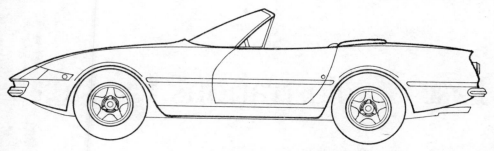

Figure 40 Ferrari 365 GTS/4 Daytona Spider, 1973

to expose the lamps; the side and direction-indicator lamps are moulded into the forward edge and flank of the front wing panel, and the air intake for the radiator comprises a slot above and below the front bumper. The broad-spoked light-alloy wheels, complete with triple-eared knock-off hub caps, not only look good but more importantly they maintain a relatively low wheel weight and assist in the provision of adequate brake cooling. Unlike the Jaguar XK120 the design of the Daytona makes no pretensions towards a strong wing line, indeed the shape is fundamentally common to the majority of present-day very high-performance cars since experimentation (by means of a wind-tunnel and high-speed track testing) has determined that this shape possesses inherent aerodynamic stability, a factor of primary importance where speeds of 150 mph and over are envisaged.

In conclusion, the Daytona Spider combines the old-established facets of a sports car with a dramatically enhanced but safely accomplished speed range (circumstances permitting). In effect it is a road-going racing car.

List of illustrations for Part 1

List of illustrations for Part 2

137

List of illustrations for Part 2

List of illustrations for Part 3

Index

Automobile body design